1966

may be kept

The Poetic Imagination of Georges Bernanos

The
POETIC
IMAGINATION
of
GEORGES BERNANOS

An Essay in Interpretation

by Gerda Blumenthal

The Johns Hopkins Press, Baltimore

To my mother
and
to G. P.

Preface

Georges Bernanos, whose stature as one of the great French writers of the 1930's and 1940's has been steadily confirmed over the past fifteen years both in Europe and South America, is only just beginning to stir the imagination of the public and critics in this country. To a large extent the paucity and, except for one or two works, the poor quality of the translations thus far available account for the time lag. It seems curious that, on this side of the Atlantic, Bernanos is still shied away from as a writer of strictly special—that is, Catholic—appeal, whose novels make sense only within the specifically Catholic framework of thought and must, hence, bewilder the uninitiated. In reality, the great Bernanosian themes—of Satan's strangle hold on the contemporary world, of death and corruption, childhood and sanctity, suffering and redemption—have become compellingly real to many thousands of readers, Christian and non-Christian alike.

What is the secret of their appeal? What is there about these works that makes an indelible impression on the imagination even before the rational mind is prepared to consent to them or quarrel with them? This is what I set out to clarify for myself, having myself come under their spell as far back as 1948. A number of critics have in recent years concentrated on the theological dimension of Bernanos' works and on clarifying the writer's major themes.

Several of these studies are marvelous. I have lived with them over the years as I have with the works themselves, and the insights they have given me have become so much a part of my own that I find it impossible at this point to acknowledge my debt to them specifically. I have listed these works in the bibliography. There is however another, better reason why I may find little or no reason to refer to earlier critical studies in the body of this essay. It is that my approach has diverged basically from the approach of those who have preceded me.

I propose to examine that secret element in Bernanos' novels which I have suspected all along of being the major source of their power, and which has not yet to my knowledge been dealt with: the superb poetic conception that both contains and transcends Bernanos' overt themes. In Bernanos' fictional universe, the poetic substance not only is inextricably interwoven with the writer's prophetic and deeply Christian insight into the shape of man and the world, but it alone gives to that insight its extraordinary vibrancy. The Bernanosian vision may invite doubt on the level of theological argument, but the truth inherent in the elemental power of its symbolism and in its flawless coherence is incontrovertible to the imagination. Its power of persuasion is that of great art. If I succeed in elucidating the poetic conception that underlies Bernanos' dramatic plots, this essay may help, however modestly, to right the balance and to vindicate, against those who might be tempted to overemphasize either the purely theological or the polemical side of the writer's fiction, Bernanos the poet.

I should like to express my warm appreciation to Mr. Howard Webber, Editor-in-Chief of The Johns Hopkins Press, for encouraging me to undertake this study; to Dr. Daniel Z. Gibson, President, and Dr. Robert Kirkwood, Dean of Washington College, for generously granting me a

leave of absence and financial aid to write it; to Mrs.
Madeline Smith, for assisting me in preparing the manu-
script; and, not least, to my family and friends who have
cheered me by their faith that the essay would turn out.
If it hasn't, it is decidedly not their fault.

G. B.

Chestertown, Maryland

CONTENTS

Introduction

The immense drama of salvation which unfolds throughout Georges Bernanos' works, from the early *Dialogue d'ombres* through the novelist's last and most complex novel, *Monsieur Ouine*, is conceived poetically as a contest between two elements, water and earth. The most persistently recurring Bernanosian image of man's tragic quest for Paradise is an unfathomable sea, on which a vessel—emissary of earth and symbol of both the protagonist and all humanity—is steadily being pulled off its course in pursuit of an unknown yet clearly divined destination. This destination is the Father's Kingdom, the "land of fountains" where a blighted earth will at last have regained access to the life-giving springs of divine love which were lying buried in its depths and have been restored to fruitfulness. However, the vessel is no sooner launched in its pursuit of Paradise than we see it arrested and engulfed by a water which reveals itself to be, ironically, not the "azure spring" of the saving water of grace but the satanic water of death in the form of an all-engulfing flood of savage, primordial power.

The deep ambivalence of the Bernanosian water expresses poetically the two spiritual poles between which the human earth is suspended in the novelist's universe and tossed back and forth: the infinite source of divine love, beginning and end of all creation, which keeps the finite and vulnerable earth young and enables it to produce ever-new forms of life; and the "thirsty water" of satanic hatred which seeks to undo the earth by first assaulting it violently, then engulfing it in mirages, and finally pulling it back into the uncreated abyss.

The symbolism is a deeply organic and coherent one. It represents a reality all at once cosmological, spiritual, and psychological. We see the Bernanosian contest between God and Satan for possession of the world and of man taking place in an earth whose springs of life have been laid bare to Satan's thirst by the Fall and have become subject to the sea's contamination. In veritable biblical floods, we see the precious living forms of creation swallowed up by the vengeful water and creation itself returning to nothingness. But above all, the Bernanosian shipwrecks testify to the human spirit's deep vulnerability to the infinitude of the sea—realm of the fallen Angel—and, on the psychological level, to the vertiginous dream of death, through which Satan lures the weary quester of Paradise back into the abyss of unconsciousness.

The failure of the two Mouchettes, the little one of the *Nouvelle Histoire* as well as her older namesake in *Sous le Soleil de Satan*, or of the myriad other children whose quest for a promised land we see arrested and subverted, invariably takes the form of a shipwreck. A small boat capsizes in a whirling storm and disappears from sight. The children's frailty and helplessness as they struggle to withstand the treacherous undercurrents of the sea are accentuated by the sinister bulk of the rotten old vessels that hover over them and in the wake of which they are trapped and engulfed. The most remarkable instance of the ubiquity of shipwreck is the satanic spell which Ouine, that "rotten old vessel which finally opens up to the sea,"[1] casts over the

---

[1] *Monsieur Ouine*, p. 222. (Pagination of all works of Bernanos recorded in the notes refers to the French editions listed in the bibliography.)

boy Steeny. The boy has hardly taken off along the "open roads" of which he has been dreaming, which will lead him to his lost father and to freedom, when his longing is subverted into a passive surrender to the liquid paradise held out to him by the false father, Ouine. Most of Bernanos' children never reach shore or even manage to drift for long. Before they can feel the ground under their feet, find the open path and face its glorious challenge, they are overcome by the violence which bears down on them from all sides and surrender in weariness to the water's magic promise of peace.

The transformation of the children's prophetic dream of life into a dream of death characterizes what Bernanos conceived to be the almost inescapable tragedy of childhood and, hence, of man. Save for a miracle of grace of which the *Journal d'un curé de campagne* is the artist's most perfectly realized poetic vision, the Bernanosian dream of Paradise, of an earth transfigured by love's *gouffre d'azur*, is turned into an evil dream of water that draws the child into Satan's *abîme de néant*. His children's dream of taking possession of the Father's Garden, of wrestling with the earth passionately and without fear and breaking a path through it, is subverted into an irresistible longing to cease struggling and to sink back into the untamed and inimical sea. Ironically, as I will show, the children drown in the water's satanically reversed reflection of the very Paradise which they have sought. In novel after novel, we see the water tending its mirror to a weary host of children and adolescents, gently dissolving a reality which is too harsh for them to endure. In the mirror of still, deep lakes, the solid walls of the earth, or of its subsidiary image the ship, which in their anguish these children see as a prison that holds them captive, become fluid expanses of gleaming shadows, promising infinite liberation and expansion; for in the Bernanosian cosmos, "the world of evil faces the world of grace as its reflection does a landscape at the edge of a dark, deep water."[2]

The number of drownings, actual or metaphorical, which the novelist depicts is deeply significant. Bernanos' fascination with water, so striking at first in a writer who has, as few others, celebrated the glory of earth's "mysterious roads, those roads filled with the steps of men . . . our roads, the roads of the world,"[3] confirms on the deepest level of the creative imagination "the ferocious irony of truth" that underlies his tragic conception of man and his fate. It is that at the very heart of a world on the march toward the Kingdom of God, and most particularly in the soul of man himself, the Usurper is at work. With wrathful vigilance he exerts his immense power to arrest the dynamic movement of a steadily unfolding creation and to reverse the divinely inspired *élan* in which man and his earth struggle toward fullness of being in the Father by tempting them to turn back on themselves and slide or "return" into the unredeemed and hence deadly abyss.

Just as the *vertige* of death and states of bleak despondency never ceased to assault the writer himself in his life and to test with nagging persistence his extraordinarily vibrant and childlike faith, so in his poetic vision man's active, virile quest to build the path through the earthly reality of self, time, and place that will lead to the Kingdom is at every moment threatened by the temptation to give up in revulsion and to surrender to the vertiginous appeal of the sea. The duel between the two movements of opening out and blossoming and of closing in and "returning" to nothingness constitutes the fundamental Bernanosian dramatic conflict. The more passionate the protagonist's pursuit of the "azure gulf" for which he is thirsting, the

[2] *Journal d'un curé de campagne*, p. 172.
[3] *Ibid.*, p. 336.

more overwhelming in moments of exhaustion is the
shadowy lure of the water which Satan holds out, as
Donissan, the novelist's most dauntless figure, confirms
with terror: "Will each of us forever see behind him, when
he turns his head, his shadow, his double, the beast that
resembles him and has been watching him in silence?"[4]
Time and time again, Bernanos' protagonist finds himself
face to face with his double, that satanic reflection of himself which attracts him irresistibly. Whereas his vision of
the goal—the desolate human landscape redeemed by grace
and become a flourishing land of fountains—has steadied
him and deepened his resources, so the backward glance of
self-reflection pries him loose from reality and pulls him
back, unknown to himself, into the enveloping slumber and
darkness of the world's and his own origin.

The lure of this backward glance is Satan's greatest
triumph. In the Bernanosian drama, it is the triumph of the
tomb over creation, of the infinite, inimical water over
earth. The sea, invading the thirsty earth in the guise of a
water of life, drinks it, in a demonic reversal of the water's
role, until all is dissolved. Bachelard, in discussing this
dissolving power of the sea in the life of the imagination
which at certain moments threatens the most solid and
hopeful souls, gives a description of it—without any refer-
ence here or elsewhere to Bernanos' works—that characterizes most aptly the movement of several works I shall
deal with at length, in particular the *Nouvelle Histoire*:
"What dissolves first [he writes] is a landscape in the rain;
features and forms melt. But little by little the entire world
is gathered in its water. A single element has taken over
everything."[5] In these works, the landscape, which is almost invariably the impoverished mining country of

[4] *Sous le Soleil de Satan*, p. 150.
[5] Gaston Bachelard, *L'Eau et les rêves* (Paris: Corti, 1942), p. 125.

Bernanos' native Artois, is leached, washed out. First lashed by rain and storm, symbols of Satan's fury, it gradually yields to the rising water until, in the end, its fragile protagonist, the child, vanishes in the caressing waves of a small pond.

The sea's destructive impact on earth takes another, seemingly opposite, form: alternating with the slippery, washed-out countryside and gently capsizing vessels that tend to prevail in the Bernanosian landscape, we find parched deserts and sinister battleships. In striking contrast to his defenseless dreamers who are most vulnerable to the appeal of the water, Bernanos has conceived his towering creatures of earth who defy the water altogether. Their response to the dangerous currents of the sea which they feel rumbling underneath is one of monumental self-defense. Here the protagonist, rather than run the risk of capsizing in the perilous pursuit of the Father's Garden, immures himself tightly within his own walls and seeks to keep himself afloat by means of a relentless vigilance that will shut out the feared element and preserve intact his embattled enclave. But this rigid divorce merely postpones the satanic water's triumph, and virtually assures it. The protagonist's endeavor to keep himself safe from the water's assault by the solidity and strength of his own finite resources alone invites disaster, for it shuts off the very springs of his life. After a prolonged suspense, in which the reader sees him already marooned in his fortress but still towering over the heaving mass of small vessels with seemingly impregnable strength, cracks begin to become visible. They grow larger and deeper until, all of a sudden, the entire giant structure breaks under its own weight and collapses into the sea. In contrast to those who, like Mouchette, are "born under the sign of dream" and tend to succumb to the water's enticements, the too-solid creatures of earth are destroyed by their resolute hostility to the element which in the Bernanosian cosmos reflects the transcendent reality of the spirit. By refusing to accept the risk of death, symbolized by the sea, which alone could lead them to a new birth of spirit and into a full flowering of life, they condemn their inner being to a barrenness that is defenseless against the rising tide of satanic hatred. In the tragic story of his great renegade priest, the Abbé Cénabre, which unfolds through *L'Imposture* and *La Joie*, Bernanos unmasks the delusion which underlies Cénabre's defiant rejection. For a while his hero is sustained by the illusion of living as he casts his shadow over the lives of others; but actually his proud autonomy is tantamount to a state of arrest in which the ground of his being is slowly washed away by a rising flood of terror and self-hatred, until it is reduced to a hollow counterpart of the Usurper's own insatiable ennui. In the end, he is forced to see himself exiled by his very pride from the land of fountains and condemned to perish from thirst in the desert, in contrast to the poorest nomad evoked in *Saint Dominique*, whose arduous pursuit of the live-giving spring keeps him alive and headed toward abundance:

> Le pauvre nomade, au coeur de ses déserts de sable, dressé à disputer au sol, pour lui et ses bêtes, un mince filet d'eau bourbeuse, a peine à croire qu'il est toujours un pays des fontaines, et que ce sera de nouveau pour ses lèvres et ses mains ce jaillissement glacé, ce bondissement plein d'écume et d'azur.[6]

Only the intercession of two of the novelist's most overflowing vessels of grace, the Abbé Chevance and his spiritual daughter, Chantal de Clergerie, saves Bernanos' towering giant of earth from complete annihilation.

[6] *Saint Dominique*, p. 10.

Between the two most destructive forms of water and earth—namely, the untamed flood, instrument of Satan's thirst, and the rocklike figure of a Cénabre, whom we see alternately as a marooned, tomb like ship and as a petrified black tree trunk towering over a parched landscape—the Bernanosian imagination, consistent with the artist's tragic awareness of the pervading devastation wrought on the human soil by Satan's hatred, has evoked swampy, washed-out country roads along which the foot seeks in vain for purchase and villages that appear buried under layers of dust. The former reflect those blurred and curiously androgynous characters whose personalities we see slowly dissolving in the liquid false-paradises of alcohol, dope, or simply their own phantasies; the latter provide the background for the host of shriveled "stumps of men" whose measure the artist took so relentlessly with a mixture of horror and pity. Between the evil infinity of the untamed sea and the pathetic finiteness of a barren, unwatered soil, the great bulk of Bernanos' humanity appears simply to miss its challenge and goal and to suffer an ignominious "return."

Yet as one drop of pure water is sufficient to purify an ocean,[7] a handful of exquisite figures conduct the Bernanosian ship to shore or, in the complementary metaphor, struggle to probe the soil more and more deeply until they strike and release the deep springs of living water. The images of a Donissan standing unflinching at the ship's prow in *Sous le Soleil de Satan* and of the unforgettable figure of Mouchette's mother steering the "sinister galley" which all are rowing, "facing the wind and at each renewed assault of the sea spewing out the bitter foam,"[8] are paralleled by that of the curé d'Ambricourt exhausting his

[7] Bachelard, *L'Eau et les rêves*, p. 194.
[8] *Nouvelle Histoire de Mouchette*, p. 133.

strength in trying to break through the hard crust of his parishioners' suspicion and greed and wondering:

> Les géologues nous apprennent que le sol qui nous semble si ferme, si stable, n'est réellement qu'une mince pellicule au-dessus d'un océan de feu liquide et toujours frémissante comme la peau qui se forme sur le lait prêt à bouillir. . . . Quelle épaisseur a le péché? A quelle profondeur faudrait-il creuser pour retrouver le gouffre d'azur . . . ?[9]

In passing unharmed across the sea and in releasing the hidden fountains in the desert, these children of grace free both water and earth from the curse of death. Through them, Georges Bernanos expresses his hope for man. In the wholeness of their being, they are men in the full biblical sense of the word. They are like masterpieces of clay, firm yet pliable, strong yet tender, which resist both dissolution and petrifaction and at the same time respond to the slightest touch of their creator. Few as they are, they bind the world together, keeping the road open and mankind on the march toward the Kingdom.

[9] *Journal d'un curé de campagne*, p. 96.

> *Si je marche à ma fin comme tout le monde, c'est le visage tourné vers ce qui commence, qui n'arrête de commencer, qui commence et ne se recommence jamais, ô victoire! Chaque pas en arrière me rapproche de la mort, ou de ce qui est à peine permis d'appeler de ce nom, la seule que puisse redouter un homme libre, dont le Christ a brisé les chaînes—la fatalité des vies manquées, perdues, le destin, fatum—toutes les fatalités ensemble, celles du sang, de la race, des habitudes, et celles encore de nos erreurs ou de nos fautes, la Fatalité à quoi nul n'échappe qu'en se jetant en avant.*

Les Enfants humiliés

I.

The Drowning of the Children

"I don't know for whom I write" Bernanos recorded in 1940, in a mood of deep despondency over the fate of his country and his own solitude and struggles in Pirapora (Brazil), where he had gone with his wife and six children in 1939—"but I know why I write. I am writing to justify myself. In whose eyes? . . . In the eyes of the child that I was. I don't care that he has ceased to talk to me. I shall never resign myself to his silence but will keep on answering him."[1] Clearly, what childhood represents here to the aging writer, and what it represents throughout his works, is above all else a challenge: the child's dauntless dream of storming Paradise and its prophetic vision of man as a saint and hero demand to be realized.

[1] *Les Enfants humiliés*, p. 195.

1

L'illusion est un avorton de rêve, un rêve nain . . . et moi, mes rêves, je les voulais démesurés—sinon, à quoi bon les rêver? Et voilà précisément pourquoi ils ne m'ont pas déçu. Si je recommençais la vie, je tâcherais de les faire encore plus grands, parce que la vie est infiniment plus grande et plus belle que je n'avais cru, même en rêve, et moi plus petit. J'ai rêvé de saints et de héros, négligeant les formes inter-médiaires de notre espèce, et je m'aperçois que ces formes intermédiaires existent à peine, que seuls comptent les saints et les héros. Les formes intermédiaires sont une bouillie, un magma—qui en a pris au hasard une poignée connaît tout le reste, et cette gelée ne mériterait pas même de nom, si les saints et les héros ne lui en donnaient un, ne lui donnaient leur nom d'hommes. Bref, c'est par les saints et les héros que je suis, les héros et les saints m'ont jadis rassasié de rêves et préservé des illusions. . . . Ce sont mes rêves qui me nourissent. . . . c'est dans la main de mes héros que je mange mon pain.[2]

All of Bernanos' images of childhood in its first un-troubled aspect of innocence, hope, and eagerness are images of springtime and transparent mornings, of freedom and departures along familiar, open paths leading to "unknown seas."

Ces routes changeantes, mystérieuses, ces routes pleines du pas des hommes. . . . Quel enfant pauvre, élevé dans leur poussière, ne leur a confié ses rêves? Elles les portent lente-ment, majestueusement, vers on ne sait quelles mers inconnues, ô grands fleuves de lumières et d'ombres qui portez le rêve des pauvres![3]

Life itself is glorious to the child, who sees it as a challenge to wrestle with, as a gateway to mysterious, hidden lands of joy. "I always forge straight ahead," Steeny boasts proudly to his little friend Guillaume in *Monsieur Ouine*. "If life is only an obstacle to overcome, I go right through

---

[2] *Ibid.*, pp. 199–200.
[3] *Journal d'un curé de campagne*, pp. 336–37.

it and come out on the other side all foaming and bloody."[4]
One of the most glowing evocations of this first reckless
launching of children into life occurs in a passage of the
Journal d'un curé de campagne. We see the curé d'Ambricourt riding down the road behind Olivier de Mainville on
the latter's gleaming motorcycle. Unexpectedly, the short
ride sums up for him all the poignant beauty of his youth
that he himself has never seen before: the purity and force
of its *élan*, its blissful disregard of obstacles, and above all
its effortless passage, right in the heart of the familiar
landscape, into "another world."

> La longue descente à laquelle nous faisions face a paru bondir
> derrière nous tandis que la haute voix du moteur s'élevait
> sans cesse jusqu'à ne plus donner qu'une seule note, d'une
> extraordinaire pureté. Elle était comme le chant de la
> lumière, elle était la lumière même, et je croyais la suivre
> des yeux dans sa courbe immense, sa prodigieuse ascension:
> Le paysage ne venait pas à nous, il s'ouvrait de toutes parts
> ... ainsi que la porte d'un autre monde.[5]

The essential role of childhood in the Bernanosian novel
lies not in its actual accomplishments—only the saints and
heroes can hope to redeem the children's overwhelming
dream of a world made whole again and restored to the
Father—but rather in the undistorted image it places before man of his essential frailty or poverty, and of the
"supernatural adventure" which he must consent to and
undertake if his life is to come to fruition. The children's
unquestioning faith in the reality of their dream of Paradise
and in the roads that promise to lead them there offers in
exemplary fashion the key to man's fulfillment. Undaunted
by the limitation of their own earthly being, they spontaneously refer their dreams and desires to a Father with

---

[4] *Monsieur Ouine*, p. 39.
[5] *Journal d'un curé de campagne*, p. 289.

whose help nothing is impossible. Like a spring soil waiting for rain and ready to burst into full bloom, they intuitively realize and accept their absolute dependence on their father's love. The child's lack of self-reflection allows his eyes to remain focused on the Paradise that beckons to him and to set out in search of it without faltering. The world through which his pursuit will lead him appears to him as open and accessible as his father's garden.

But here the great Bernanosian tragedy begins. No sooner do the children come face to face with the world in a first *prise de conscience*, at the critical moment of adolescence, than they are stunned and arrested by its chaos and violence. Far from reflecting a father's love, it reveals itself to be an alien and hostile landscape in which an impoverished and barren soil vainly defends itself against the assaults of a heaving sea. The human soil or ship whose function it is to sustain the children in their perilous quest for the Father fails them miserably; the sea is the huge "jaw of death" in which the false father and Prince of the World is waiting to trap them at the moment when they recoil in terror from the wilderness before them.

There is a deep and characteristic link in the Bernanosian crisis of late childhood or adolescence between its earthly dimension—the psychological and social elements which induce the first violent recoil—and its satanic—in which the child's terror is turned into despair and he is drawn into the abyss. In a movement that accelerates ominously, we see one flowing and expanding into the other. The human or existential phase is marked by roaring confusion and violence, its satanic climax, in contrast, by motionless silence.

The first sign which suggests to us that Bernanos' children, in entering the contemporary arena of life, are entering a desolate and cursed realm is that all of them are orphaned, either physically or psychologically deprived of a father. Philippe and Olivier in *Un Mauvais Rêve* are bastards; the father of the little Mouchette is a drunkard and misfit; the fathers of Evangéline (*Un Crime*) and Philippe (*Monsieur Ouine*) have mysteriously vanished; and those of the big Mouchette, of both Chantals, and of many others have simply abdicated or never even recognized their parental responsibility. The novelist is merciless in his indictments of the mentors of his "lost generation," who not merely fail to steady the children at the moment of greatest danger but actually pull the ground from under their feet. The society into whose hidden chaos the children find themselves thrown abounds in signs of aberration and decrepitude—spiritual and moral, psychological and physical. It is both mired in hypocrisy and self-delusion and petrified by greed and pride. Anxiously defending its security, founded on money and power, against the children's vibrant dreams, it not only views these with secret rancor but has set to exploiting them savagely for its own ends. "We are here like wise men among the insane," Philippe remarks bitterly to Olivier in *Un Mauvais Rêve*. "For the old are insane, I am positive, old age is madness. . . . All these guys are old, regardless of their age."[6]

We see the children stunned by the backwash of malice and inertia that sweeps over them and thrown into a violent recoil. At that critical moment, the thirsty sea opens up under them. In a mysterious enlarging of the scene, the moral and psychological drama of arrest and revolt is transformed into an intimate confrontation between the child and the Spirit that has opposed and defied the mystery of life and creation since the beginning of time: Satan, the Usurper. The sea becomes the eye of the Antagonist who has been lying in wait and now fastens on the child. The

[6] *Un Mauvais Rêve*, pp. 28–29.

water's evil mirror seizes the child's vision of life and, reversing it into a vision of unearthly peace, draws him into the void. The spiritual shipwreck of a child, summing up as it does the Bernanosian tragedy of human betrayal and its fearful consequence, the victim's almost inevitable succumbing to the spell of the Serpent's eye, is Bernanos' most haunting and persistent leitmotif. We find it virtually in every work, if not in the foreground, then at least evoked briefly but incisively. One major work is completely focused on it: the *Nouvelle Histoire de Mouchette*, completed in 1937, a year after the *Journal d'un curé de campagne*. It is one of the writer's greatest works.

The story of the rape and suicide of the fourteen-year-old daughter of a drunkard and smuggler "who would sell her for a round of old rum,"[7] set in the desolate mining country of the Artois, has the simplicity of line and movement of a Greek tragedy. The action takes place in less than twenty-four hours and is focused entirely on the child. With the swiftness of a dream, Mouchette's course leads her, in the space of one night and a morning, from the sinister loneliness and brutality of her home and surroundings, to the sudden blossoming of her carefully guarded dream of love, to its instantaneous transformation into a nightmare of horror and shame, and finally, in the satanic transformation of this nightmare, to her encounter with the spell of death, which draws her into the water.

The crisis which decides Mouchette's fate is conceived poetically as an uneven battle between water and earth. It begins with a simple rainstorm that rips through the countryside; progresses in violence as the rape adds a new dimension of devastation to the ravages of the storm; and finally moves beyond the physical and psychological level to its satanic climax, when the ground under Mouchette

[7] *Nouvelle Histoire de Mouchette*, p. 169.

gives way completely to the dissolving waters and the child drowns. The imagery is of the most tightly knit consistency. It gives to the whole tale both that dreamlike quality which is so characteristic of Bernanos' evocations of childhood— Mouchette was born, he tells us, "under the sign of dream"[8] —and, by raising the duel between the two elements whose pawn Mouchette is to the level of a struggle between satanic wrath and human endurance, a transcendent spiritual significance.

All the participants of the drama, both elemental and human, are heard rather than seen. In evoking them as voices, that is, in the most suggestive and at the same time the least tangible mode, the novelist suggests the dreamlike nature of their impact on the child—that is, Mouchette's almost totally unconscious response to them—as well as the boundless power of repercussion which even the simplest events assume in the immense and mysterious context of a human being's destiny.

"But already the big dark wind," so the story opens, "the sea wind, as Antoine says, is scattering the voices in the night. It plays with them for a moment, then gathers them all up and throws them no one knows where, snarling with rage."[9] All the signs of childhood and growing life—spring, morning, a budding earth—are already blighted: the spring is a "desolate March," the poor, barren soil is being whipped and swamped by a driving rain.

> Le crépitement de l'averse redouble et il s'y mêle à présent l'immense chuchotement du sol saturé, les brefs hoquets de l'ornière qui s'effondre et parfois, sous quelque dalle invisible, le bouillonnement de l'eau pressée par la pierre, son sanglot de cristal.[10]

The image of the battered soil sums up with great power the besieged state in which we first encounter Mouchette.

[8] *Ibid.*, p. 209.   [9] *Ibid.*, p. 1.   [10] *Ibid.*, p. 15.

She is near the end of her rope[11] and about to founder in the swamp of loneliness, destitution, and cruelty in which she has been struggling to get her bearings. Ashamed of her miserable rags and awkwardness, the child has been the butt of her classmates' taunts and of the ill-concealed contempt of the schoolmistress and has, through daily exhausting efforts, managed to withstand their assaults on her pride by assuming a posture of scornful defiance. Underneath this rigid posture, maintained at the price of a growing anguish, she has kept buried her only source of hope and solace: a poor child's dreams of strange lands, full of love and joy. But just like the saturated soil which is unable to resist any longer the dissolving might of the hostile element, the child's defenses have begun to give way and she has let her enemies pry out of her the treasure which has sustained her. The deep chest-voice which she has assumed, in defiance of the schoolmistress' insistence on her "taking an interest in music," has several times in her despair yielded to a limpid, crystalline voice, rising suddenly "as if out the depths of a magical, impenetrable night." This voice expresses her whole being—its radiant, inviolate purity and its ardent expectation. In a highly significant metaphor, its rising to the surface is seen as the emergence of "a tiny barge on the crest of a mountain of foam."[12]

The first move of the precariously suspended little barge in the swiftly unfolding story is a blind move of distress. Terrified equally of the malice and hypocrisy of her schoolmates and of her father's cowardly brutality at home, the child is seen running through the woods after school has let out, driven by a blind desire to escape and be free. As she runs "the ground closes in over one of her shoes, with an

[11] "Nous sommes tous au bout du rouleau," Ganse says in *Un Mauvais Rêve*.
[12] *Ibid.*, p. 6.

awful lapping noise."[13] Suddenly, Arsène, the young poacher, stands before her.

> Le vent semble venir de tous les points à la fois, et il se creuse çà et là, au plus épais du taillis cinglé par la monstrueuse averse, de véritables tourbillons.[14]

The motif of the rushing whirlpools at the appearance of Arsène announces a new peril. To the lonely Mouchette, this man whom she has been watching for some time from a distance has become an idol. He is the one human being who, in his reckless defiance of the law, represents to her the strength and freedom which she has found missing in everyone else. He has become the living embodiment of her dreams. In her need and awe of him, the ordinarily deeply withdrawn girl is ready to trust him blindly.

In a development of poignant irony, Arsène takes the drenched Mouchette to his hut to protect her from the downpour. "Come on in. . . . the water is rising."[15] As she dries herself by the fire he has made and drinks a few sips of his sour wine which burns her empty stomach, her first feeling of panic yields to drowsiness and exhaustion. Outside, "the wind redoubles in strength. A livid sky flows above their heads, with the huge rumbling of swelling waters."[16] The apparent safety of the poacher's hut quickly reveals itself to have been a delusion. The short moment of respite merely marks the subtle transition in which the girl is led from the *ivresse* of her own solitude and anguish into the more treacherous *ivresse* of the drunken Arsène's stories. "It's a cyclone, my girl," he says to her, and then to impress her tells her of a cyclone he once was in. Its description is an exact symbolic representation of the child's impending destruction:

[13] *Ibid.*, p. 16.   [15] *Ibid.*, p. 25.
[14] *Ibid.*, p. 20.   [16] *Ibid.*, p. 26.

Il s'est fait un grand silence, puis la mer, du côté du nord-
ouest, figure-toi, la mer s'est mise à bouillir. Oui, tu aurais
dit l'eau d'une casserole lorsqu'elle commence à chanter. . . .
Et voilà que le toit des docks s'est soulevé lentement, lentement. De loin, ça ressemblait à une bête qui se gonfle, un
dragon. Puis, la voilà encore, cette sacrée toiture, qui bat
comme une voile, et monte dans le ciel, avec la charpente,
vrac! . . . Quand le cyclone a passé sur la ville, la terre a
tremblé. Mais dans ce cas-là tu ne sens pas la force du vent:
elle aspire, tu es dans le vide. Tu n'entendrais même rien du
tout, n'était les briques des faîtes, les ardoises qui pètent de
toutes parts, un vrai feu de salve. La ville et la mer fumaient
ensemble.[17]

Something, an "imperceptible crack in his voice," warns
the girl that the poacher is drunk, but already she is spellbound. Her admiration for him deepens when, having gone
back into the woods to find her lost shoe, he returns and
tells her that he has killed the forest warden Matthieu in a
fight. As he draws her into his confidence, enlists her help
in establishing an alibi, treats her as an equal and a partner,
her smothered dream of love breaks through, this time to
full consciousness. Again it finds expression through song.
As she sits and watches tenderly over the poacher who has
dropped to the floor in a violent epileptic fit, she begins to
hum softly. Slowly her voice rises, until it becomes a spring
of living water in which her blighted little being at last
unfolds.

Et tout à coup elle chanta. . . . Sa surprise fut si grande
d'avoir cette fois surmonté sa crainte qu'elle l'emporta
d'abord sur tout autre sentiment. Elle écouta jaillir cette
voix pure, encore un peu tremblante, d'une extraordinaire
fragilité. Aucune expérience préalable ne lui permettait de
comprendre que cette voix mystérieuse était celle de sa
misérable jeunesse soudain épanouie, une revanche d'hu-
miliations si anciennes que sa conscience les acceptait telles

[17] *Ibid.*, pp. 30–31.

quelles, y trouvait parfois son repos, une inavouable douceur. Cette voix était son secret. Le seul qu'elle pût partager aujourd'hui avec le bizarre compagnon étendu à ses pieds, vivant ou mort, mort sans doute. . . . Et maintenant qu'elle avait livré ce trésor, elle ne le reconnaissait plus. Elle écoutait son chant avec une humble ferveur, il rafraîchissait son corps et son âme, elle eût voulu y tremper ses mains.[18]

In a passage of less than fifteen pages, Bernanos evokes with extraordinary imaginative and dramatic intensity the turning point of his heroine's fate: her rape by Arsène. The rape theme constitutes the basic Bernanosian theme of satanic thirst: the outflowing movement of love in which the deepest springs of life have begun to exert their creative power is brutally reversed by an invasion of hatred. Poetically, this reversal is conceived as a flood in which the ocean's polluted water sweeps over the soil and washes it away. It is a "cyclone" more vicious than any the girl has yet experienced, and it leads directly into the final movement of her foundering.

"Abruptly the magical voice ceased."[19] Arsène has recovered consciousness and suddenly looms over her, bringing her sharply back to reality. He is still in a daze and looks at her suspiciously, trying to reconnect the threads of what has happened. The child reminds him of the murder and, as he does not seem to recall killing the warden, begins to press him anxiously. To her, the crime is precious, since it makes her her hero's accomplice and offers her a chance to help him and perhaps even save his life. The effect of her insistence is fatal: trapped in his lie, the muddled and still drunk man turns on her like a wild animal.

The ravaging effect of his vicious assault, which takes place in silence and darkness, is reflected in the forest.

[18] *Ibid.*, pp. 74–77.   [19] *Ibid.*, p. 88.

Mouchette lies motionless on the ground, blindly seeking refuge in the soil. But "the sand, washed out by the rain, sinks under her weight, and she almost completely disappears in it."[20] All around her water is glistening.[21] When she finally gropes her way home along the trail, like a wounded animal which, with muscles tensed by the terror of death, seeks in vain to save itself from the "hounds' jaws," the trail is so washed out that, instead of running, she has to slide down its slope. "At last she let herself slide to the bottom."[22]

The movement of capsizing and sinking gains momentum throughout the second part of the book. Mouchette, when she finally reaches the old, weatherbeaten hut, finds her mother near death. The mother's final agony, which consummates a lifetime of patient and exhausting struggle against misery, both physical and moral, serves to push the child more deeply into her relentless confrontation with death and to lay bare before her eyes the ocean's elemental fury that has already dashed her hopes. Just before the mother dies, we see Mouchette clutching at the last remaining sign of life within her reach, as she picks up her screaming and hungry baby brother "with the unconscious movement of a drowning man who is going under."[23] With her mother's death, Mouchette's last real support vanishes, not only against an alien, inhuman world but, even more important, against the water's magic spell which is beginning to approach her. The final glimpse we get of the mother is of an earthbound being whose solidity and endurance have withstood the fiercest assaults of the sea. With a good earth's sturdy power of absorption she has exposed herself for all of them to the sea's bitterness and rendered it harmless.

[20] *Ibid.*, p. 77.   [21] *Ibid.*, p. 91.   [22] *Ibid.*, p. 90.
[23] *Ibid.*, p. 94.

Bien qu'elle ne s'en rende nullement compte, la vieille femme assume le poids de leur misère. Son bavardage, qui parfois les harassait tous, les longues bouderies, les colères bruyantes qui faisaient fuir jusqu'à l'ivrogne, ébahi par ce déluge de mots, c'était leur voix et leur silence, l'expression vigilante, jamais lasse, de leurs âmes taciturnes, le témoin du malheur commun, et de la part qu'il comportait d'humble joie. Et c'était aussi leur révolte. Sur la sinistre galère qu'ils ramaient ensemble, la mère était la figure de proue, face au vent, et à chaque nouvel assaut de la mer, crachant l'écume de l'embrun.[24]

The child vaguely discerns that she has been the victim, not even of a man, but of a dream, a drunken man's dream. The night's "cyclone" was nothing more than a storm, she is told, and no one was murdered. But her despair does not turn her against her deceiver. Ironically, because of the absolute character of the child's dream of perfection, "M. Arsène remains exactly where her admiration has placed him, once and for all, once and forever. Oh cursed childhood which does not want to die."[25] This last is probably the most sorrowful sentence Bernanos ever wrote.

In a characteristic movement of recoil, the child's shame and revolt "already turn against herself, it is herself that she hates."[26] In struggling to keep intact the image of her ideal by seeing herself as unworthy of it, she herself makes possible the final phase of her destruction. "She is obeying a law as fixed and implacable as the law governing the fall of bodies; for a certain despair has its own acceleration. Nothing will stop her now: she will go to the end of her misfortune."[27] In the gloomy morning hours which correspond to Mouchette's "cursed childhood," the sounds of rain and storm give way to the silence which marks the dead center or eye of a cyclone.

[24] *Ibid.*, p. 133.   [25] *Ibid.*, p. 110.   [26] *Ibid.*, p. 154.
[27] *Ibid.*, p. 156.

We see Mouchette, who has left the hut early in the morning after her father has come home drunk, slipping through the streets of the village in a daze. A blind impulse leads her to the warden's house, there to confirm to herself, by seeing him alive, "the hideous error on which has foundered all in one blow her youth, her real youth, which only yesterday was ready to emerge from childhood, to be born. . . ."[28] The voice of the warden who questions her about the poacher sums up all the brutality of a world in which there is no place for children and no more place for her.

> Il l'appelle tout de suite, de cette voix qu'elle redoute entre toutes, qui réveille d'un seul coup ses terreurs d'enfant, la voix commune à tous les subalternes de la grande armée de la loi, une voix qui ressemble un peu à celle du guignol des ducasses, pleine d'une bonhomie féroce.[29]

As her last efforts to steady herself by defying first her father, then the warden, and finally the villagers rebound against the impenetrable walls of their malice and indifference, her movement of "return" gains its final impetus. "It was in going back through the village that the idea came to her."[30] This mysterious sentence introduces the last part of Mouchette's story: the child's surrender to the dream of death in her bizarre, phantasylike encounter with the *veilleuse des morts* and her suicide in the tiny pond by the quarry.

The figure of the old *veilleuse des morts*, whose house turns out to be the destination of Mouchette's dazed return through the village, is a personification of the satanic *abîme de néant*. Prefiguring Ouine, she has about her something of the serpent's eye which takes hold of the child in despair and subverts its dream of life into a vision of peace, purity, and stillness. She begins to talk to the child about

---

[28] *Ibid.*, p. 113.   [29] *Ibid.*, pp. 158–59.   [30] *Ibid.*, p. 172.

the dead whom she watches during her long nightly vigils. "In the old times, they say, people worshipped the dead, the dead were gods! That should be the true religion, child. Everything living is filthy and stinks."[31] As Mouchette sits opposite her, "the pale blue eyes fix her with an irresistible expression of curiosity, compassion, and an obscure, inexplicable complicity."[32] Under the spell of this gaze, which seeks to draw out her "secret," the child feels her power of resistance dissolving. She sinks into a void in which she hears only the slow, hypnotic ticking of a clock.

> La vieille s'est assise en face d'elle, sans mot dire. L'horloge . . . bat lentement, pesamment, et à chaque descente du balancier de cuivre jette un éclat sur le mur. Un moment, Mouchette essaie de lutter contre ce silence, mais elle s'y est prise trop tard sans doute, il monte, il l'enveloppe, elle a l'impression que la nappe invisible recouvre ses épaules, son front. L'illusion est si forte qu'elle croit faire pour se débattre, échapper, un immense effort, et cependant elle est incapable de bouger. Au moment même où elle cesse de lutter, se laisse couler à pic, elle entend de nouveau la voix de la vieille qui a l'air de poursuivre une phrase commencée:
> —Tu n'es pas dans ton bon sens. Patiente un peu, ma belle, reste ici.
> —Non, fait Mouchette, faut que je rentre.
> —Pas sur tes jambes, alors! Tu ne peux pas te tenir debout. Le silence monte de nouveau, mais cette fois Mouchette ne lui oppose aucune résistance, au contraire. Elle s'y laisse tout de suite glisser avec un frémissement de tout l'être, qui est presque un frémissement de bonheur.[33]

The old woman takes a dazzling white sheet from her linen closet and offers it to the girl for her mother's burial. "Suddenly the idea of death merged with the image of those piles of immaculate sheets."[34] In a demonic reversal of life and death, of height and depth, the white gleam of the

[31] *Ibid.*, p. 186.   [32] *Ibid.*, p. 179.   [33] *Ibid.*, pp. 180–81.
[34] *Ibid.*, p. 185.

sheets becomes "another source of light, incredibly gentle,"[35] whose serenity and radiance eclipse the daylight, shut out by the drawn curtains.

The *veilleuse des morts* finally succeeds in drawing out of the child the secret of her shame. "By what sorcery? For words would not have sufficed to open this contracted heart and release the source of tears."[36] Through the reflective power of the serpent's eye, the child's still unconscious despair is made lucid and instantly overwhelms her. We have here the consummation of the rape theme: the only powerful defense of childhood—the unconsciousness of its suffering, which preserves it from measuring the depth of its fall or the distance which separates it from its goal—is destroyed by the satanic invitation to see and to know. The ensuing *vertige* of consciousness is fatal.

> Elle savourait maintenant ce dégoût avec une lucidité qu'elle n'avait jamais connue, qui lui paraissait merveilleuse. La vieille sacristine a dit les paroles qu'il fallait, les seules qui pussent attendrir Mouchette sur elle-même! Et . . . voilà qu'elle songeait à sa propre mort, le coeur serré non par l'angoisse, mais par l'émoi d'une découverte prodigieuse, l'imminente révélation d'un secret, ce même secret que lui avait refusé l'amour.[37]

The two aspects of the evil dream, conscious hatred of self and of life induced by self-reflection, and its counterpart, the mirage of deliverance, merge, as the child who has lingered for a while on the edge of the pond by the deserted quarry surrenders to the "voice" of the water.

> Le "à quoi bon?" la question terrible, inexorable, à laquelle nul homme réellement passionné n'a pu répondre et qui a décidé du salut de quelques rares héros par un miracle de grâce, car elle se retourne d'ordinaire contre celui qui le prononce, symbole de l'antique serpent, ou peut-être le

[35] *Ibid.*, p. 184.   [36] *Ibid.*, p. 204.   [37] *Ibid.*, p. 205.

serpent lui-même, n'arriva pas jusqu'à ses lèvres. Elle se posa au-dedans d'elle, informulée, ainsi qu'une mine qui éclate dans l'eau profonde, et dont l'oreille n'a perçu que le sourd grondement, alors que la houle irrésistible monte déjà de l'abîme muet.[38]

The final image of the drowning child "gently pivoting on her side"[39] suggests a capsized ship. A small detail recapitulates the bitter irony which condemns Bernanos' children to a swifter and more complete destruction than any of his adult figures: it is by throwing her head back and "gazing at the highest point of heaven" that she goes under. The gesture is symbolic of the children's impetuous longing to storm paradise *hic et nunc* and of the satanic counter-movement which it unleashes: the surging hatred that prevails on life to return to nothingness.

La même force de mort, issue de l'enfer, la haine vigilante et caressante qui prodigue aux riches et aux puissants les mille ressources de ses diaboliques séductions, ne peut guère s'emparer que par surprise du misérable, marqué du signe sacré de la misère. Il faut qu'elle se contente de l'épier, jour après jour, avec une attention effrayante, et sans doute une terreur secrète. Mais la brèche à peine ouverte du désespoir dans ces âmes simples, il n'est sans doute d'autre ressource à leur ignorance que le suicide. . . .[40]

[38] *Ibid.*, pp. 216–17.   [39] *Ibid.*, p. 223.   [40] *Ibid.*, p. 217.

II.

Rotten Vessels

The process of dissolution and liquefaction is nearly ubiquitous in the Bernanosian universe. The drowning of the children is its most violent and sudden manifestation; but perhaps more sinister are the innumerable instances in which we see characters and places disintegrating slowly, as if infected by some form of cancer or gangrene. They begin to swell up, ooze water, gradually lose their shape, and finally turn into porous, amorphous masses which sink to the bottom of the sea.

In the seemingly chaotic but actually superbly controlled movement of *Monsieur Ouine*, this deadly process occurs in its full range and is tracked to its origin, which forms the novel's largely invisible center of gravity—the thirst of the satanic water, in the form of the infinitely active, mesmerizing glance of Ouine. Through this glance, which becomes one with the satanic eye of the sea, Bernanos evokes the sea's ultimately futile yet ruinous craving to usurp the divine "secret" of life by drawing it out of the living creatures of earth. Here, in contrast to the *Nouvelle*

18

Histoire, this rape is conceived as a slow, insidious invasion and pollution of the earth's life-giving springs by the destructive water, as a result of which aberrant, tumorous growths start mushrooming all over with irresistible force.

In the microcosm of Fenouille, the reader encounters all at once a landscape, its dwellings, and its people in that putrid stage of decomposition in which water seeps out everywhere and the air is filled with an evil smell. Bernanos referred once to his extraordinary last novel as "Job's dungheap" and a "lugubre urinoir."[1] This is at least on one level a very apt description. Torrential rains are, throughout the novel, washing out roads, rotting pastures, and swelling the pond in which the little cowherd is found dead. Black water seeps from under the stone floors of the castle—symbol of Fenouille's nobility—and gives to the room in which Anthelme de Néréis is dying the "living force of certain plant leprosies."

> Loin de la détruire, il semble que l'eau ne ferait qu'en gonfler la semence, profondément enfouie sous pierre.[2]

The pillars of its sacred place, the dark and dank church, "sweat out an icy, stagnant water which makes the hands greasy."[3]

The evil water has contaminated the population, right down to the children, to the point where Steeny himself, the key figure among the novel's all-important three children, suddenly sees himself in despair as a contaminated well:

> . . . une part de lui-même avait été, lui vivant, frappée de mort, abolie. Par quelle blessure mystérieuse, par quelle brèche ouverte de l'âme avait-elle glissé au néant? Il

---

[1] Albert Béguin, *Bernanos par lui-même*, p. 166.
[2] *Monsieur Ouine*, p. 82.
[3] *Ibid.*, p. 158.

semblait qu'avec elle se fût évanouie toute sécurité, toute
certitude et que la conscience, ainsi qu'une citerne crevée
ne laissât plus désormais monter à la surface qu'une eau
limoneuse, chargée d'angoisse.[4]

Finally, and above all, there is Ouine himself, the "soft and
humid" false father of Fenouille, whose bone structure has
disappeared "as if his skin no longer covered anything but
a sort of soft fat"[5] and who in dying resembles "a rotten
old ship opening up to the sea."[6]

Water and death are linked inseparably in this work.
There appears to be no trace of a pure spring left in
Fenouille, the "dead parish." Hence the mayor's despond-
ent reflection, near the end of the novel, that water is
powerless, that only fire can put an end to the mire which
has swamped the village. "There is no filth, no smell that
can resist fire. We don't know of any water that's as pure
as fire, right? . . . I should have known that water could do
nothing to help me, that there is nothing better than fire."[7]

Yet ironically, and here lies the profound originality of
this work, the poisonous miasma which rises from the soil
to breed violence, insanity, and death in Fenouille, derives
its deadly power from a calm, icy *abîme de néant*, in which
a great dreamer of purity, Ouine, has taken refuge from the
impurities and the turbulence of earth.

The antagonist's basic motif, the great satanic motif that
Bernanos develops in *Monsieur Ouine*, is the spirit's revulsion at the *souillure* of incarnate life—its weight, its smells,
its share of death and corruption. Like the fallen Angel to
whose spell he has succumbed, Ouine is offended by the
scheme of creation in which spirit and finite, mortal matter
are linked indissolubly. He refuses to wrestle with the to
him despicable "fatalities" of existence and chooses instead

[4] *Ibid.*, p. 121.   [5] *Ibid.*, p. 226.   [6] *Ibid.*, p. 222.
[7] *Ibid.*, pp. 203–4.

to vindicate his dream of Paradise in his own fashion, by circumventing them. In his bitter hatred of the earth, he has detached himself from it by assuming the role of an outsider, or stranger, a dispassionate, benign spectator not subject to its contamination. His retreat is evoked as a deliberate gliding down to the depths of the sea, where none of the shocks and reverberations which agitate the earth are felt and where his defiant spirit can observe and taste life in a state of purity, in the water's magic mirror.

"I no longer meet anything head on," Ouine confides to Steeny in their first encounter, in which he imparts to the boy his loathing of all living things and their ineradicable tendency to deteriorate and die. "Like those living jellyfish at the bottom of the sea, I float and absorb."[8] One may question Bernanos' discretion in attributing this savage perception of himself to Ouine—here as elsewhere, the writer's imagination has run ahead of the possibilities of dialogue—but the image itself is significant. Slippery and effeminate, the old language professor has repudiated the active, masculine effort of facing up and giving shape to the world and appears indeed hardly to stir from his peaceful abode, the little pink room in the Néréis' castle. At the same time, in order to satisfy his obsessive thirst for life—characteristic Bernanosian symptom of a being submerged by satanic hatred—he has become an infinitely active extension of the Serpent's eye which feeds on the lives of others.

Ouine is the prototype of all of Bernanos' satanic figures. Himself seduced in his childhood by a false father figure, one of his teachers, he has in turn become a vengeful seducer. Unlike Mouchette, he has survived the blight of his childhood's dream of Paradise and is maintaining the illusion of living by feeding on the substance of other living

[8] *Ibid.*, p. 25.

beings, whom he in turn is able to entice away from their love of earth and into the deep waters of satanic hatred. Through the power of his glance, Satan's bottomless reaches of nonbeing absorb the earthbound reality of life and simply dissolve it.

Throughout the novel, the fundamentally ambiguous, counterfeit nature of this glance, which is the secret of the antagonist's power of seduction, is accentuated. As Ouine's name suggests, he destroys what he appears to affirm. Just as water reflects the landscape at its edge in reverse, so Ouine, the false priest of Fenouille, is a counterfeit figure of love and innocence. His sexual ambiguity—does he rape the little cowherd? was he ever in love with Jambe-de-Laine?—suggests childlike innocence. His unctuous manner suggests the priest; his detachment from worldly concerns, the poverty and selflessness of the saints. Above all, his "passion for souls" is a cruel counterfeit of a father's love. Whereas the vision of a Donissan, a Chevance or a curé d'Ambricourt encompasses in a flash the mysterious struggle of a soul in distress, orients it anew towards its goal, and reconciles it to itself, that is, *inspires* it, Ouine's avid eye arrests its victim in an ironic reflection which reveals to the latter all his latent *dégoût* and self-hatred and, thus overwhelming him, sucks him in or *l'aspire*. The anguished and warped inhabitants of Fenouille—Bernanos' greatest evocation of the modern world in its state of inner disarray—are an easy prey for Ouine's mesmerizing glance. They open themselves up to him and, as they surrender to his gaze their deepest terrors, find not only themselves emptied of the last vestige of pride and purpose which has sustained them but the world of others turned into a chain of tarnished mirrors endlessly reflecting their own hateful self-image.

Il ne dit jamais de mal de personne, et il est très bon, très indulgent. Mais on voit au fond de ses yeux je ne sais quoi qui fait comprendre le ridicule des gens. Et ce ridicule ôté, ils n'intéressent plus, ils sont vides. La vie aussi est vide. Une grande maison vide, où chacun entre à son tour. A travers les murs, vous entendez le piétinement de ceux qui vont entrer, de ceux qui sortent. Mais ils ne se rencontrent jamais. Vos pas sonnent dans les couloirs, et si vous parlez, vous croyez entendre la réponse. C'est l'écho de vos paroles, rien de plus. Lorsque vous vous trouvez brusquement en face de quelqu'un, il n'y a qu'à regarder d'un peu près, vous reconnaissez votre propre image au fond d'une de ces glaces usées, verdies, sous une caresse de poussière.[9]

Ironically, the treacherous glance which is thirsting for its victims' "secret," that is, the mysterious spring of life which is the source of the created world's beauty and vitality, is debarred from what it craves by its very act of invading and polluting it. What it takes hold of time and again is not the human earth's sublime though vulnerable creative *élan*, its divine gift, the promise of Paradise, but only their reverse: earth's dream of death, and its longing to return to the uncreated abyss. It is ultimately in vain that Ouine, after having induced in his victims a *vertige* of self-hatred and scorn of earth, holds out to them a dazzling reflection of the sea, in which the tasteless and colorless "thirsty" water of the abyss takes on the vibrant beauty of a redeemed and purified earth. To this reflection they succumb. But the beings whom his satanic glance succeeds in absorbing so disintegrate in the process that they bring nothing to fill the gaping emptiness. Their vital substance is simply lost, lost both to creation and to Satan whose thirst it cannot but cheat by its elusiveness. In the dying Ouine's monologue which, near the end of the novel,

[9] *Ibid.*, p. 218.

Steeny hears in a prophetic dream that marks the boy's liberation, Ouine is forced to face up to the divine irony whereby the deceiver must in the end see himself as deceived: in defying his earthly condition and seeking Paradise in the water's unbounded realm of reflection—symbol of the Serpent's false promise of power and immunity—he has permitted himself to be dissolved into nothingness. He has become no god but a mere mirror of the Serpent's vacant, craving eye.

> La curiosité me dévore. . . . A ce moment elle creuse et ronge le peu qui me reste. Telle est ma faim. Que n'ai-je été curieux des choses! Mais je n'ai eu faim que des âmes. Que dire faim? Qu'est-ce que la faim? Je les ai convoitées d'un désir, auquel le mot faim ne convient pas, la vraie faim grince des dents, le regard de la faim brûle comme du feu. . . . Je les regardais jouer et souffrir ainsi que celui qui les a créées eût pu les regarder lui-même. . . . je me sentais leur providence, une providence presque aussi inviolable que l'autre. . . .
>
> Ai-je vraiment fait ce que je viens de dire? . . . L'ai-je seulement voulu? L'ai-je rêve? N'ai-je été qu'un regard, un oeil ouvert et fixe, une convoitise impuissante?[10]

Nevertheless, the impact of the satanic eye on the human landscape is ravaging. Out of the depth of the earth and its inhabitants, Ouine's glance draws forth a veritable flood of malice and hatred in which the entire village is caught up. Each seeks to rid himself of his own unbearable ennui by foisting it on others, until Fenouille's population becomes

> . . . ce lac de boue toujours gluant sur quoi passe et repasse vainement l'immense marée de l'amour divin, la mer de flammes vivantes et rugissantes qui a fécondé le chaos.[11]

The first major victim of the satanic spell which Ouine's eye has cast over Fenouille is the possessed creature who is

[10] *Ibid.*, pp. 241, 242.
[11] *Journal d'un curé de campagne*, p. 172.

the village's *châtelaine*. We learn that Jambe-de-Laine—the villagers' injurious nickname for Mme. de Néréis—installed Ouine in the château shortly after her marriage to the weak, sensuous Anthelme de Néréis and has been serving him with slavish devotion. Revolted by the baseness and vulgarity of the village into which she has come to live as a result of her marriage, she sees in the serenely detached Ouine a kind of avenging deity who will obtain retribution for her and bring her into a purer, calmer world:

> . . . quiconque l'approche n'a justement plus besoin d'aimer [she tells Steeny], quelle paix, quel silence! L'aimer? Je vais vous dire, mon coeur: comme d'autres rayonnent, échauffent, notre ami absorbe tout rayonnement, toute chaleur. Le génie de M. Ouine, voyez-vous, c'est le froid. Dans ce froid, l'âme repose.[12]

The sign that she has been caught in the icy depth of Ouine's satanic hatred—"A clear and icy water, that is what hatred is," she tells the boy—is the "magic glance" by means of which she in turn draws out of her husband and all the young men who have succumbed to her spell their basest impulses.

Drained of her joy and will to live by her satanic master, Jambe-de-Laine has become another link in the chain of the *abîme's* reflections, another unfathomable eye condemned to invade and to "drink" with satanic glee the poisoned source of the lives of others. ". . . there is enough substance in a single man to feed a whole life—and what life can boast of having drained another to the end, to the bottom, to the dregs?"[13]

But something is still alive in Jambe-de-Laine and stirs violently. Unlike Ouine, whose motionless fluidity suggests the final stage of earth's return to water, the figure of the

[12] *Monsieur Ouine*, p. 88.
[13] *Ibid.*, p. 89.

châtelaine is seen oscillating between the water's deadly magic and an authentic struggle for life. Her "incredibly pure profile" reveals vestiges of great nobility; her demented bearing suggests a mortally wounded creature's last effort to wrench itself free of the trap. We see her alternately as a spider, a wild beast, a monstrous broken toy, a creature pursued by ghosts, but most significantly "a trapped animal . . . which, after a night, a day, and another night of immense effort, having dragged behind it the trap and chain, faces the always fatal second dawn and, though still on its feet, enters the death agony."[14] These images, and the symbolic wild mare behind which we see the *châtelaine* careering down the roads, in their ambivalent evocations of both a destroyer and a victim, confirm Jambe-de-Laine's deeply equivocal role in the novel. She both defies life by serving Ouine and throwing herself and her victims into his avid *gueule*, and in turn, in moments of clear-sightedness, she hates and defies the evil old man and finds the strength to denounce him and warn his victims of the snare. This ambivalence manifests itself most clearly in her relationship to Ouine's choicest prey, the boy Steeny.

The special object of the antagonist's gaze, in this novel again, is a child. The child is not only the most defenseless victim; he is, above all, the purest embodiment of the secret of life which the Serpent has forfeited and seeks in vain to recapture. Significantly, the novel's violent but at first hidden movement of fermentation erupts into the open after the central event has taken place: the unaccounted-for rape and murder of the little cowherd whom Ouine has sent off in the night with a message to Steeny's mother and followed and who is found the next morning naked and strangled in the pond. "Childhood is the salt of the earth," Ouine exclaims with great emphasis after the funeral. "Let

[14] *Ibid.*, p. 82.

it lose its savor, and soon the world will be nothing but rot
and gangrene."[15] No sooner, indeed, has the child been
buried, than murders, suicides, and insanity sweep through
Fenouille. At last the mayor himself becomes insane with
self-loathing and fear and vanishes from the scene. The fate
of the children in the novel's "world of old men" is the most
haunting theme of *Monsieur Ouine*, but that is at least in
part because it is related so closely to the inevitable decay
of a world that does not treasure and protect its children.
Despite all appearances to the contrary, it is their innocence, Bernanos keeps reminding the reader, which is
holding the world together and keeping it from turning back
on itself completely. Whereas we see the rest of the village's
inhabitants arrested and mesmerized by their own image
reflected in Ouine's glance and pulled back into the fundamentally inhuman, anonymous *dégoût*, or hatred of life,
which is like the backwash of the stream of creation, the
children's quest of the Father's Kingdom is a movement
accomplished in blindness to themselves and in a clear,
intuitive discernment of the goal. After the little boy's
funeral, Ouine has indeed reason to gloat and to assume,
with ill-concealed satisfaction, that Fenouille has been left
defenseless against its inner pollution: "It would now produce poison with anything, the way diabetics produce
sugar."[16]

The young priest echoes the sinister prophecy:

> Vous verrez surgir de toutes parts des maires de Fenouille
> qui tourneront contre eux, contre leur propre chair, une
> haine désormais aveugle, car les causes resteront enfouies
> au plus profond de la mémoire héréditaire. . . . Au train où
> va le monde, nous saurons bientôt si l'homme peut se ré-
> concilier avec lui-même au point d'oublier sans retour ce que
> nous appelons de son vrai nom l'antique Paradis sur la terre,
> la Joie perdue, le Royaume perdu de la joie.[17]

[15] *Ibid.*, p. 169.   [16] *Ibid.*, p. 168.   [17] *Ibid.*, p. 208.

However, two children are left in Fenouille after the cowherd's death: Guillaume and Steeny. Both are fatherless and, in an almost all-encompassing sense, disinherited. They have nothing to sustain them but each other's friendship and the unfulfilled promise of their dream of Paradise. Yet such is the power of their dream and of the mystery of life which they incarnate that in the end it breaks the Serpent's snare and turns his triumph into defeat. First shocked into an awareness of the true nature of Ouine's "calm" water by the little cowherd's violent death, Steeny, on whom we see Ouine's glance fasten in an attempt at seduction that now has all the dimensions of the Bernanosian satanic rape, is able to overcome the antagonist. Even in this work, in which the writer puts before us his most disconsolate vision of the world as a "dead parish," rotting in self-exile and unable to draw pure water from any source, the source is there. The children, both living and dead, continue to point the way. The dramatic and poetic core of *Monsieur Ouine* is very clear: it is the critical encounter between the serpent, Ouine, and a dove, in the figure of the adolescent Philippe or Steeny, whose eager, pulsating life is caught, early in the novel, in the cold depth of Ouine's glance and who very nearly perishes in it.

Every character, episode, and image in the novel bears directly on the boy's fate. From the opening pages, the stage is set for an overwhelming drama, in which the virile, heaven-bound spirit of the boy is setting out to discover and join his missing father—human correlative and symbol of the divine Father—and is almost turned back by the effeminate, dissolving spirit of fear and death. We see that spirit close in on the boy through a chain of satanic eyes or mirrors that extends from his mother to the governess, to Jambe-de-Laine, to the host of corrupt and cowardly villagers, to Ouine's glance, which is the "jaw" of death.

We find the boy brooding in a house which, in the absence of his father who long ago disappeared mysteriously, has been transformed by his mother into a jealously guarded island which will preserve her from the "perfidious water" of the sea. Her infallible weapon against the challenges and perils of living is an evasive gentleness that absorbs every active force and reduces it to impotence.

'La douceur a raison de tout.' . . . Et c'est vrai que rien n'a résisté à cette douceur, jamais. . . . Comment ne pas l'imaginer sous les espèces d'un animal familier? Entre elle et la vie, le rongeur industrieux multiplie ses digues, fouille, creuse, déblaie, surveille jour et nuit le niveau de l'eau perfide. Douceur, douceur, douceur. A la plus légère ombre suspecte sur le miroir tranquille, la petite bête dresse son museau délié, quitte la rive, rame de la queue et des pattes jusqu'à l'obstacle et commence à ronger sans bruit, assidu, infatigable.[18]

There is a muted hint that her ingenious gentleness once wove its snare of silence around the enemy of her peace, the impassioned Philippe, her husband, and destroyed him. He is "the vanished, the sunken, the eternally absent one."[19] Now she recognizes in her growing son Philippe the same hated driving force that surges ahead, threatening her tranquillity, and she is calmly determined to defy it again in him. Everything about the house is stifling the boy. It is indeed the very negation of a "father's house"—"Why do guys always talk about their father's house?"[20] he wonders. It has become a gilded cage, a Lesbian love-nest for the two women from which the world, and the boy in particular, are subtly excluded.

The dual theme of the boy's dream of finding his father and his almost instant arrest is stated immediately and forcefully. We see Philippe, or Steeny as his mother calls

---

[18] *Ibid.*, p. 4.   [19] *Ibid.*, p. 3.   [20] *Ibid.*, p. 44.

him to blot out his father's memory, immobilized by terror as the insinuating glance and the sly hands of Miss, his mother's companion, take hold of him and seek to provoke him to punishable aggression. He wrenches himself free, crying: "No! No!" Sick at heart, he looks out of the window, longing to escape and to go off in search of his father whom, despite what he has been told, he firmly believes to be alive. But all he can see is the tiny village and, beyond it, "the tiny yellow road, coiled in on itself like a snake and leading nowhere."[21] He is ready to do anything, throw himself into any breach, only to be free and set out on his search. At that moment, as if summoned by magic, Jambe-de-Laine appears and invites him to visit her guest, Ouine, at the château. As the boy, who is perplexed by her unusual appearance but delighted to be able to escape, gets into her carriage and they race towards the to him unfamiliar place, he wonders, with a strange sense of foreboding, where this adventure will lead him, *"vers quelle fatalité?"*[22] The child's foreboding turns out to be well founded. The image of the circular road prefigures the satanic snare into which his blind revolt is throwing him. The paternal, slightly ridiculous figure of the old professor, who, puffed up with fat despite an advanced case of tuberculosis, welcomes him in the little pink room in the château, is the satanic shadow or double of the father the boy is searching for and now believes he has found.

Ouine's concern for him is but a thinly disguised craving. For years, he confides to Steeny, he has been watching the boy from a distance, longing to know him:

Que de fois je vous ai vu traverser la route pour monter vers Hagron en tuant des merles! Et du premier regard j'avais reconnu cette marche inégale, tour à tour impérieuse ou lente, et ces sursauts que vous avez, comme d'un appel

[21] *Ibid.*, p. 9.   [22] *Ibid.*, p. 15.

augural, ces haltes brusques, absurdes en plein soleil . . . ah!
c'était bien bien là l'image que j'ai caressée tant d'années,
une vie, une jeune vie humaine, tout ignorance et tout
audace, la part réellement périssable de l'univers, seule
promesse qui ne sera jamais tenue, merveille unique![23]

To Ouine, the boy represents his own lost childhood and its
glorious promise. "I have just seen myself again," he has
told Jambe-de-Laine, "as a dead man sees the past. The
little boy I once was, I have seen him, I could have touched
and heard him."[24]

In a satanic movement of repetition and reflection, Ouine
now fastens on the boy the same gaze his own seducer once
fastened on him—"on his own glance that of another,
unknown, empty and fixed as that of a dead man."[25] As
Ouine talks about life with the boy, a sense of enchantment
overcomes Steeny. He feels far removed from everything.
The imagery of the passage evokes the satanic metamorphosis of solid walls into an enveloping, caressing tide:

Le merveilleux silence de la petite chambre paraît seulement s'ébranler, virer doucement autour d'un axe invisible.
Il croyait le sentir glisser sur son front, sur sa poitrine, sur
ses paumes ainsi que la caresse de l'eau. A quelle profondeur
descendrait-il, vers quel abîme de paix? Jamais encore au
cours de cette journée capitale, il ne s'était senti plus loin
de l'enfance, de l'univers maintenant décoloré de l'enfance,
des joies et des peines d'hier, de toute joie, de toute peine.[26]

Reading bitterness and defiance in Steeny's eyes, Ouine
begins a discourse in which this defiance is projected and
magnified to a point where it becomes an overwhelming
defiance of life itself. Everything in life, he tells the boy, and
youth in particular, ends up corrupted and destroyed
because life is nothing but a process of decay, a return to
nothingness.

[23] *Ibid.*, p. 25. [24] *Ibid.*, p. 87. [25] *Ibid.*, p. 147.
[26] *Ibid.*, pp. 21–22.

> Tout s'altère, se corrompt, retourne à la boue originelle. . . .
> Ah! Philippe, chaque pas que vous faisiez en avant, sous
> l'averse de feu, *chaque pas que vous faisiez le soir au-devant*
> *de votre ombre*, arrachait de moi une crainte, un scrupule. . . .[27]

As the boy listens in awe and drinks glass after glass of the
Madeira which his host keeps pouring for him, the shadow
of death spreads over him in the form of Ouine's huge
silhouette on the wall. Throughout the novel, his hovering
shadow signifies the child's ensnarement by the intoxicating
dream of water. Under his false father's shadow, he feels
immune: nothing can touch him any longer, nothing matters. "Oh absurd dream!—Steeny thought he had found the
predestined companion of his life, the initiator, the hero
whom he had pursued through so many books." He is
"drunk with overcome pain, security, and pride."[28] In
Ouine's presence, life is seen as hideous, but it no longer
has the power to hurt him.

> Philippe croyait sentir, non sans un vague effroi, le même
> silence se refermer autour d'eux, silence vivant qui paraît
> n'absorber que la part plus grossière du bruit, donne l'illu-
> sion d'une espèce de transparence sonore. Car c'est bien en
> effet, à la magie de l'eau, à ses souples enveloppements, un
> miracle éternel de l'eau que rêve Philippe.[29]

That night Steeny falls asleep in Ouine's room. In the
deeply organic universe which the Bernanosian vision
evokes in this work, in which no part of his teeming human
landscape is touched without setting off deep reverberations
throughout the whole, the triumph of the satanic dream of
returning to death is confirmed by the murder that takes
place that same night of another child, the little cowherd.
It is a pitch-black night in which "torrents of water" inun-
date the roads and the cowherd loses his way to the village.
The next morning,

[27] *Ibid.*, p. 25. Italics mine.   [28] *Ibid.*, p. 19.   [29] *Ibid.*, p. 23.

. . . la même pluie lourde, sans aucune brise, tombait
d'aplomb sur le sol fumant. Très loin, vers l'est et comme
au bord d'un autre monde, l'aube orageuse formait lentement ses nuées, à travers une poussière d'eau.[30]

Ironically, Ouine's strangle hold on the boy tightens
progressively as the grim reality of the "perfidious water"
and of living beings putrid with inner corruption impinges
more and more strongly on Steeny's aroused consciousness.
He sees Anthelme dying from a gangrenous infection, which
is but an outer manifestation of the nobleman's weak and
dissolute being, and he learns, first from the dying man and
then from Miss, the truth about his father's fate. It is
worse than death: after having been believed dead for five
years, the father was found in an asylum in Germany and
simply left there. He either became insane or was locked
up for desertion in the war. In keeping with the novel's
over-all character of an unsolved riddle, the father's fate is
not fully clarified for the reader. All that is certain is that
he is one of Bernanos' unforgiven and unforgiving "dead,"
whom human cruelty and indifference have simply erased
from the earth and thrown into the deep sea of oblivion,
from which their dream of revenge keeps rising to poison
the living. Guillaume, the crippled boy to whom Steeny has
run early in the morning, unable to bear the horror of what
he has heard and seen, reflects on the curse which seems to
lie on the village. In a penetrating vision, he sees these
unloved dead and their aborted lives, who have been claimed
by the abyss, tugging at the earth from below with hatred:

Le désordre universel, s'ils en étaient la cause? Moi, je les
vois très bien à la frontière qu'ils ont franchie trop tôt,
malgré eux, et qui s'efforcent de la repasser—les coups qu'ils
portent ébranlent le monde.[31]

[30] *Ibid.*, p. 31.   [31] *Ibid.*, p. 48.

Guillaume, whose intuitive perception is re-enforced by a passionate devotion to his friend, warns Steeny of the backwash of hatred and self-repudiation to which his father and his whole lost generation who served as cannon-fodder in the war have succumbed and to which Steeny has now been left prey.

> Votre avidité, votre dureté, votre passion de revanche—cette rage à vous contredire, à vous renier, comme si vous aviez fait déjà de grandes choses, des choses mémorables, et qu'elles vous eussent déçu. . . . Tenez, votre admiration pour M. Ouine, votre idée d'un héroisme à rebours. . . .[32]

But the successive revelations of evil have overwhelmed Steeny. He is unable to face up to them, even with the support of his little friend who urges him "never to turn his head back, but only to think of tomorrow." In a highly symbolic passage, we see him caught that day in a suicidal *vertige*, in which his and Guillaume's dream of heroic conquests and discoveries is defeated and transformed into the consoling vision of Ouine's aquatic paradise.

Prompted by his own intuition and his friend's warning, the boy tries to resist his new hero and take flight. He begins to dream of the open road, symbol of human striving and hope.

> La belle route! la chère route! Vertigineuse amie, promesse immense. L'homme qui l'a faite de ses mains pouce à pouce, fouillée jusqu'au coeur, jusqu'à son coeur de pierre, puis enfin polie, caressée, ne la reconnaît plus, croit en elle. La grande chance, la chance suprême de sa vie est là, sous ses yeux, sous ses pas. Brèche fabuleuse, déroulement sans fin . . . arche sublime lancée sur l'azur. . . . Qui n'a pas vu la route à l'aube, entre ces deux rangées d'arbres, toute fraîche, toute vivante, ne sait ce que c'est que l'espérance.[33]

[32] *Ibid.*, p. 40.   [33] *Ibid.*, p. 71.

"Today . . . today," it tells him. But another voice answers, "Why not tomorrow? Tomorrow would be too late. . . . In twenty-four hours, one could lose his life, he said to himself in a state of intoxication." He is arrested by a vivid hallucination in which the "radiant image of death" holds out to him "a brand new, shining life—untouched, immaculate—miraculously restored to him."[34] At that very moment, Jambe-de-Laine's wild mare comes racing straight toward him and misses him by the breadth of a hair. Everything begins to whirl around him: the road slides into a heaving sea.

> La route s'est mise à remuer doucement, doucement sous lui, ainsi qu'une bête dorée . . . tout ce qu'il peut faire, mon Dieu, c'est de garder son équilibre, de tenir en équilibre, sur ses épaules, cette tête vide. . . . Peine perdue! C'est tout le paysage à présent qui glisse jusqu'au creux de la houle, chavire.[35]

The novel's pervasive theme of human betrayal and corruption and their impact on the boy, whom they threaten to deliver into the satanic snare set for him by Ouine, are sharply restated in this episode by means of a metaphor. A former woodcutter of the forest of Saint-Vaast happens to witness Jambe-de-Laine's assault on the boy, in which, we gather, she is simultaneously trying to kill the boy and to destroy herself in order to put an end to her sinister bondage to Ouine. Both the *châtelaine* and Steeny are depicted metaphorically in the young trees of the exploited and devastated forest:

> La vieille forêt vendue, revendue, vendue encore, passant de mains en mains au fond d'études sordides et tout à coup, son sort fixé, jetée bas en vingt semaines, écrasée, broyée, débitée par trains entiers jour et nuit, jusqu'au dernier

[34] *Ibid.*, p. 72.   [35] *Ibid.*, pp. 77–78.

charroi triomphant à travers le village, la musique, les drapeaux, puis le silence qui retombe sur les jeunes taillis éventrés, tout nus, grelottant au vent d'hiver. . . .[36]

After this episode, which leaves the boy weak with terror, the focus shifts back to the village, which is described as "stewing in its crime." It appears to be unable to purge itself of the evil that has taken possession of it, as any healthy organism would, even a large city which "when night falls sweats out through all its pores the filth of the day that has ended and sweeps it into its ditches and gutters, until it becomes one slimy mass slowly flowing out to sea through its immense subterranean rivers."[37] The rancor of the village keeps rising. Suspicion falls on the young poacher and son-in-law of Vandomme, Eugène, and he is arrested and charged with the child's murder. Drawn with obvious love, this Eugène is one of Bernanos' high-spirited young rebels, who appear predestined to serve as scapegoats for the world's rotten old men. Unable to prove his innocence, challenged by his stiff-necked old father-in-law to save the honor of the family, Eugène, together with his young wife Hélène, commits suicide in his hut the night before the arrest. The death of these two is characterized by the same movement of gliding and sinking we have seen in the *Nouvelle Histoire*. Here again, it marks the trans-formation, through despair, of the vital, impelling dream of Paradise, of an earth redeemed by grace, into the engulf-ing dream of death.

. . . j'ai rêvé tous ces temps-ci [Hélène tells him] d'une grande forêt très haute, rien que des troncs comme des colonnes, tout droits, tout noirs, et je croyais voir la mer à travers, très loin, une grange bleue. . . . Du moins, je croyais que c'était la mer, puisque je ne l'ai jamais vue.[38]

[36] *Ibid.*, p. 75.   [37] *Ibid.*, p. 163.   [38] *Ibid.*, p. 152.

But when she is on the point of pulling the trigger in despair, she surrenders to a water which is no longer the azure gulf, reward for an accomplished journey, but a deep place of refuge from a world that is unbearably evil:

> Jamais elle ne s'était sentie plus molle, plus souple, toute docilité, toute caresse. Il lui semble qu'elle flotte sans pesanteur au fond d'une eau calme où nul remous ne peut l'atteindre. La pensée même de la fin prochaine ne lui parvient qu'amortie et décolorée à travers cette épaisseur limpide. Ah! faire vite ce qui doit être fait, glisser de cette paix dans l'autre. . . .[39]

The double suicide of the young people is conceived, much like the cowherd's murder for which in a mysterious way it serves to atone, as an immolation. It is another slaughter of innocents by the village, intended to appease the satanic storm that has caused its "lakes of filth" to overflow. But with every victim it devours the water keeps rising; its thirst appears bent on absorbing and dissolving all that is still intact. On the day of the child's funeral the crowd's malice reaches its height in the presence of the small white coffin which finally confronts it tangibly with its own pollution. The priest's glance tries in vain to rest on a solid face or shape in the vast heaving mass in front of him: everywhere it slips.[40] In the cemetery, the crowd is a "somber flood." "With the roar of waters when the sluice gates are opened,"[41] it closes in, first on the priest, almost pushing him into the freshly dug grave, then on Jambe-de-Laine. She dies a few days later, more, we are told, of her own will to die than of the physical injuries they have inflicted on her.

The *châtelaine's* death, like that of the two Mouchettes or of Eugène and his wife, places us before one of the central mysteries of the Bernanosian drama: these suicides

[39] *Ibid.*, p. 153.   [40] *Ibid.*, p. 167.   [41] *Ibid.*, p. 174.

are in reality murders. In destroying themselves, the victims of satanic violation or rape merely consummate the destruction wrought on them by the Antagonist. Their surrender to the water, far from expressing a rejection of the Father and of their dream of Paradise, is in fact a last desperate act of hope—hope that in destroying the hateful reflection of themselves and of the world, which they see in the sea's mirror, they will overcome the obstacle that stands between them and the Father. There is a poignant suggestion that those deaths do indeed, despite the delusion which underlies them, break the satanic mirror, with its dreadful vision of life as living death, and restore their victims to innocence. If this is so, then the thirsty water is cheated of its prey; for what awaits those children of reckless hope at the moment of death is the true confrontation they have been seeking all along: the earth's reconciliation with the *gouffre d'azur* of the Father's love, source and fulfillment of all life.

All these deaths have a redemptive function in the novel. They serve to wrench Steeny out of the jaw of death by arousing him sharply. As the boy's gaze becomes clearer and stronger, it slowly subdues the treacherous power of the Antagonist's eye, until finally the roles are reversed. In the end, it is Steeny who witnesses the defeat of his mentor. What he sees is that the only one who dies, in the ultimate sense of dissolving irrevocably into nothingness, is his "hero" himself, the murderer and usurper of life. Ouine, whose glance has fed on others throughout his lifetime, is forced at the moment of death to turn this glance on himself. What is finally revealed to him is that the life he has coveted and believes he has made his own has eluded him; that he has nothing, is nothing, and is returning to nothingness. Even Jambe-de-Laine, he bitterly concedes to the boy, has eluded him:

—Elle s'est échappée, voilà le mot, elle s'est élancée hors
de toute atteinte—échappée n'est peut-être pas le mot qui
convient? Elle s'est élancée comme une flamme, comme
un cri.[42]

At the end of *Monsieur Ouine*, a profound silence reigns
again. The satanic storm has spent itself, after unleashing
a flood of evil that has left the village devastated, and we
are back in the dead center of the storm's eye, the little pink
room where the old language professor is dying. The
tuberculosis which finally kills him is, like the tumors and
cancers that feed everywhere on Bernanos' deceived humanity, the visible sign of the encroachment of delusion on
reality, of the thirsty flood within the bowels of the earth
that, like "a life within a life," eats away the earth's
strength and substance. Now it is Steeny's turn to watch
his dying mentor with deep attention. Sober, rid of his
intoxication at last, he is able to face up to the Serpent's
eye and see it for what it is: not a haven of peace but a
roaring abyss.

Just before Ouine dies, we see the boy's release from the
professor's strangle hold and the re-emergence of the dream
of Paradise out of the depths of the dream of death. Still
spellbound by his idol and deeply grieved at the sight of
Ouine's approaching death, Steeny suddenly recalls a memory. It prefigures perfectly his impending liberation from
his false haven and the resumption of his quest for the true
Father. As he looks out of the window from Ouine's room
where he has been spending days and hours on end, he
remembers how, to escape from his mother and Miss, he
used to spend hours by the empty dovecot right by the
house. It had been closed to the birds for fifteen years.

Quinze ans! Il imaginait le départ des oiseaux, leur détresse.
Des heures, des jours, des mois peut-être, ils avaient dû

[42] *Ibid.*, p. 242.

cerner la vieille tour close de leur vol, de leurs cris, de leurs
ombres. . . . Puis ils étaient partis un matin, vers quelque
pays fabuleux.[43]

Within an hour or two after Ouine has died, the boy who
has once again had too much wine and has fallen asleep by
his mentor's bed has a final prophetic dream. In this dream,
Ouine and the Serpent are one. He hears Ouine moaning
with rage and frustration as he is sucked into the gaping
void of his own insatiable desire:

> Je désirais, je m'enflais de désir au lieu de rassasier ma faim,
> je ne m'incorporais nulle substance, ni bien, ni mal, mon
> âme n'est qu'une outre pleine de vent. Et voilà maintenant,
> jeune homme, qu'elle m'aspire tout entier, je me sens fondre
> et disparaître dans cette gueule vorace, elle ramollit jusqu'à
> mes os.
>   —Pouah! [the boy replies] vous parlez de votre âme
> comme la grenouille pourrait parler du serpent.
>   —Cet animal me fascine en effet, poursuivit imperturbable-
> ment M. Ouine. Est-ce sa faim que je sens, ou la mienne. . . .
> Oh! mon garçon, si ce n'est ici qu'un rêve, ce rêve est bien
> étrange.[44]

Among the last words that Steeny hears Ouine murmuring
"in a tone of enormous greed" are "a whole life, a long life,
a whole childhood, a new childhood."[45] In his dream, the
boy still sees Ouine's immense shadow hovering over him,
but now it fills him with "a vague, indefinable pity, with
the kind of sorrowful serenity which comes after the crisis
of a great illness, when the awaited dawn that will bring
recovery is still below the horizon."[46]

The event of Ouine's death and of the child's emergence
is summed up poetically by Bernanos in the image of a
poisonous liquid which, through exposure to the open air,
has lost its power. "The vials are empty, the poisons

[43] *Ibid.*, p. 217.   [44] *Ibid.*, pp. 234–35.   [45] *Ibid.*, p. 236.
[46] *Ibid.*, p. 237.

evaporated in the air, diluted, innocuous." The deadly water of Satan's thirst, divested of its magic, is "tasteless, colorless, neither hot nor cold . . . it would quench no fire. . . ." Ouine tells the boy in his dream, "My thirst and this water are one and the same."[47] And Steeny sees him wondering, wrathfully, who would ever want to drink this "thirsty" water with him.

[47] *Ibid.*, p. 239.

III.

The Dialogue of Shadows

One of the most dramatic manifestations of the "fierce irony of truth" through which the satanic abyss seeks to reabsorb the world of created forms is of the nature of an explosion. The "icy calm" of pure evil, that tasteless and colorless water which represents the nothingness to which Satan exiled himself by defying the divine creative will, is a state to which it is hardly given to any of Bernanos' figures to enter. Ouine is the only one whom we see literally returning to nothingness. He is the only one who appears to be beyond redemption, because there is not one grain of healthy substance left intact in him which might be nurtured by the living water of divine grace and might form the nucleus for a "whole, new life." He is the one purely satanic figure who can claim at the moment of his death that he and the "thirsty" water are one and the same.

But on a different, more earth-bound level, Bernanos has created a succession of powerful and strangely iridescent antagonists who, even though their vital resources are almost hopelessly polluted, are still engaged in an intense struggle for life. They are his thwarted artists and mystics whom we see failing in their creative role because they have succumbed unwittingly to the untamed abyss and its monsters raging in the depths of the unconscious. Instead of summoning all the vitality and promise hidden in the subjects to which their imagination is drawn, and thus truly creating them, Bernanos' deluded dreamers of redemption both exploit and suffocate their subjects in a vain endeavor to purge their own imagination of its tyrannical "evil dreams." In highly dramatic developments, we see a potentially creative process subverted into a process of destruction: the would-be creator's "evil dream" alone, that shadowy "double" of his creative vision, takes hold of the subject and so thoroughly floods it that, far from tapping a fresh source of inspiration which might restore his vigor and freedom, he finds himself face to face with yet another "shadow"—the subject's own aroused "monsters" or "evil dream." The great explosions which rock the Bernanosian universe become imminent when two darkened, "polluted springs" thus start to interact and to potentiate each other.

In at least three of his major works—the early short story, *Madame Dargent; Un Mauvais Rêve;* and, on a somewhat different level, the curious alternate version of the latter, *Un Crime*—the artist conjures up this particular manifestation of the intrusion of the satanic into the creative process. All three works are conceived as "dialogues of shadows," in which the creative relationship of master to subject has been subverted into a devastating complicity and battle between an impotent creator and his betrayed victim and accomplice. We see these dialogues attain their greatest intensity wherever a particularly vital and "interesting" subject proves both too resistant to suffer instant shipwreck as a result of violation by the antagonist and at the same time too weak to face up to the antagonist's glance openly and overcome it. In those relationships, the evil dreams of both partners mix and potentiate each other like two toxic liquids in an alchemist's test tube. The Bernanosian "dialogue of shadows" is a feverish game of cross-reflections in which each of the two participants seeks to impose on the other, and simultaneously draw out of him, his hidden "untamed beasts" of fear and horror of life and the ultimate "evil dream" of death. Like an "unnatural marriage," it is not only barren but condemned to breeding monsters.

Significantly, the two vocations whose "shadow" or satanic aspect the antagonists represent are those of the writer and the religious. Dargent is a fashionable writer of the Anatole France variety—Bernanos' *bête noire*, of whom we find another incarnation in *Sous le Soleil de Satan* in the figure of Saint-Marin. Ganse, the novelist of *Un Mauvais Rêve*, is a would-be Balzac, a kind of giant whom we encounter at a point in his career when his creative *élan* is exhausted, fighting a losing and increasingly vindictive battle against sterility. Finally, the false curé of Mégère in *Un Crime* is a feminine imposter who, unknowingly, acts out the life-long obsession of her mother, an ex-nun, with the religious vocation the latter has forfeited and who succeeds, for a few brief days, in impersonating a priest.

In Bernanos' poetic vision of a world which is ceaselessly struggling to emerge from the ocean of death and to assume the shape and form to which its divine creator keeps summoning it, the vocations of the artist and the priest play an exemplary role. They are the great creative vocations, and by that very fact also the most difficult and threatened. Their authentic realization constitutes the highest form of response to the divine challenge, the highest expression of man's own creative vision of Paradise whereby he is able, in a landscape both interior and exterior, to bring to life an abundance of flourishing and subtly differentiated forms. In Bernanos' own work we get more than a hint of the deep link which the writer felt to exist between the poetic and the prophetic function. They are virtually inseparable. One is not surprised to come upon his very personal confession that "a writer's vocation is in some cases the other side of a vocation to the priesthood."[1] Certainly in saying this Bernanos did not mean to revive the old confusion between the artist and the mystic. He simply meant that the writer who has faced up to and mastered in his own imagination the demons that threaten everywhere to turn a heaven-bound earth back into the uncreated abyss is a redeemer in his own right. He is free to give testimony to the world in a poetic vision in which every image or moment can assume a significant function in the indivisible unity of a whole, in which it can accede from the status of an isolated and deeply precarious accident to that of a vital metaphor or symbol. Bernanos clearly conceived the work of art to be in its own way a metaphor of creation, with its ardent thrust towards unity and transparency on the one hand and, on the other, its breathtaking plunges into the yet chaotic and unredeemed flood in the depths of the world and the self. "If the good Lord really wants a testimony from you," he wrote to a young writer, "you can expect to work a lot, suffer a lot, and doubt yourself constantly, both in success and in failure. Because, seen in this way, the writer's job is no longer just a profession, it is an adventure, more than anything a spiritual adventure. All spiritual adventures are Calvaries."[2]

Like Mauriac, but with freer and profounder insight, Bernanos grapples with the problem of the ever-threatening

---

[1] Béguin, *Bernanos par lui-même*, p. 149.
[2] *Ibid.*

presence of the satanic in the heart of the artist's creative struggle. It is evoked by him as the artist's own "evil dream" that surges, ironically, from the depths of his anxiety and from the bitter *dégoût* he feels in face of the human earth's unfathomable longing to "return" and submerge itself in the sea. It insinuates itself into his creative vision and submerges it in a secret aura of complicity with death, which, in turn, will extend to both his subject and his reader or spectator.

Only a heroic, because infinitely dangerous, determination to face up to the "evil dream" and strip it of its false promise can free the imagination from its bondage. The work of art, Bernanos keeps reminding himself and his fellow-artists, as Malraux was to do a few years later, is before anything else an act of the will. It is the artist's lucid response to the unfathomable powers that solicit his imagination, both divine and satanic, and his recognition that he can neither evade them nor surrender to them. He must face up to them and, by giving them form, transmute them from overwhelming sources of terror into integral elements of creation. "Are you afraid of the real presence of your demons?" he chided a young confrère. "Are you contenting yourself with the easy job of disciplining your thoughts, rather than harness your beasts, for our edification? But my dear old pal, that is the leap you have got to take."[3] In his reflections on Racine, the same thought is reiterated and amplified: all great art has its beginning in the artist's struggle with his demons. Art in its highest form is a struggle to overcome the thirsty water of the inner abyss, and a quest for being.

> On ne peut le nier: l'art a un autre but que lui-même. Sa perpétuelle recherche de l'expression n'est que l'image affaiblie, ou comme le symbole de l'Etre. Racine . . . eût-il

[3] *Ibid.*, p. 151.

atteint son point de perfection, s'il n'avait un jour, d'un
coup sublime, surmonté l'homme moral et retrouvé l'homme
pécheur? Nulle autre cause que celle-ci n'expliquerait sa con-
stante amertume, je ne sais quel frisson douloureux partout
sensible, ni le silence tout à coup gardé, ni la mort. . . . Déjà
dans le cri de triomphe et de bienvenue à la vie de l'adolescent vainqueur, aimé, célèbre, se décèle la fêlure imperceptible, le frémissement de la joie mêlée d'angoisse, la
recherche d'une vérité plus profonde. Qui le suit au long de
la route aride? Jusqu'à ce qu'ayant vu se dresser tout à
coup, engendrée de son art, pâle de la volupté pressée
jusqu'au supplice, sa petite main secrète posée sur l'épaule
de son insignifiante amie,—Phèdre,—il reconnaît le visage
fraternel et son propre remords dans les yeux mourants.[4]

The work that truly liberates its creator, his subject, and
his reader does so by dint of the lucidity and freedom which
the artist has brought to bear on his dreams; it is a triumph
of the creative will over blind impulse and obsession. If
Monsieur Ouine, for all its satanic fury, or for that matter
any other of Bernanos' unfailingly tragic works, succeeds in
giving the reader a genuine sense of redemption, it is
because Bernanos himself achieved that heroic lucidity with
regard to his own deepest terrors that enabled him to express them poetically in forms that are fully detached from
their source and are consequently able to live and testify
with the freedom of universal symbols. "For many years
[he tells us] I have not written what I have been most
impatient to write, and no doubt that is a great grace
which God has given me, perhaps the greatest. . . . I no
longer love my book when I start writing it, but I want it
with an invincible will, and if I may without being ridiculous use such an expression for works as modest as mine,
with a tragic, a naked will, which is reduced to the essential
like a landscape devoured by the sun. Yes, when I begin

[4] *Ibid.*, p. 154.

writing a book, I have been detached from it for a long time, but I write it precisely in order to recapture at all costs the lost source, the impetus of soul which gave it birth."[5]

Significantly, the dominant figures in his "dialogues of shadows" which give poetic expression to Bernanos' lifelong fear of being blinded by his own at times overwhelming terrors and of being turned unwittingly from an authentic creator into a possessed violator are not the masters but their defrauded subjects. These women embody Bernanos' parched human landscape with its perennial thirst for the redeeming springs that will restore it to life. The writer's vision reaches beyond the isolated event of the artist's own defeat: the individual creator's failure or betrayal of his vocation is seen as tragic, above all, because it entails nothing less than a setback for the whole of creation. Because of it, we see the world sliding back, though ever so little, towards the deep waters of delusion and death instead of advancing toward fullness of life.

All the dialogues' subjects are basically deeply feminine beings who long to find fulfillment in the service of a strong creative will that will save them from barrenness and shipwreck. Their tragedy is that they fail to encounter it. A false master's semblance of creative power has aroused their hope and their deepest devotion, but they soon discover that he has nothing to give them. Neither truly masculine nor feminine, he is the tyrannical and impotent partner who is unable to offer fulfillment and to create new life. All he can do is probe and experiment in order to uncover their "secret" or hidden flaw and to project into it his own obsession which he cannot master. The violated subject begins to retaliate by reflecting back to him in turn the image of his impotence. Slowly, we see an inversion of

[5] *Ibid.*, p. 150.

roles take place. The subject, after having been drained of
hope and contaminated by the poisons of the master's
frustration and his impotent attack, begins to take her
revenge. The more exhausted and effeminate he becomes,
craving more and more desperately to master his elusive
subject only to find himself increasingly at her mercy, the
more masculine the figure of his partner begins to appear.
We see her need to expel the incubus of his tormenting
dream and to free herself of it at any cost by an act of her
own free will transform her into an ambiguous figure whose
icy calm conceals a rising flood of hatred. The dialogue
culminates in an explosion in which she at last delivers
herself of their "child." That birth turns out to be a vengeful act both of destruction and of self-violation. By means
of it, she at last bests her master at his own game. The
tragic climax of the explosion is not, however, in Bernanos'
dynamic conception, a pure triumph of evil. By releasing
into the open the secret poisons of that "alchemy of evil
dreams" which up to that point has maintained a perfect
resemblance to an authentic creative process, the explosion
reveals it openly to be creation's satanic shadow or "double"
and thereby breaks its spell.

The heroine of the remarkable short story which heads
the *Dialogues d'ombres* prefigures Simone Alfieri of *Un
Mauvais Rêve*. We find Dargent's young wife near death
but unable to die. The realm of Dargent's delusions in
which for years she has been enduring a living death is
suddenly fractured by the overwhelming impact of death's
real presence. She is suspended in the agony of suddenly
"seeing" herself in an hallucinatory vision of water, in
which she finds herself face to face not with herself but
with that self's evil double, which has taken over her life
and is finally strangling her. This double is the incubus of

all of Dargent's morbid phantasies that the writer has failed to bring to life and that she, mesmerized by the glamour of his sensational, phantom-like heroines, has been under a compulsion to "live out."

> Il y a . . . une grande étendue d'eau . . . ce doit être un lac. . . . Attends. . . . Attends que je me penche. . . . Tiens-moi ferme! . . . Oh! Oh! Oh! . . . Elle pose sur lui un regard indéchiffrable, étrangement attentif et limpide, mais où passent et repassent les grandes ombres de la catastrophe intérieure.—C'est que je me suis vue, dit-elle, dans l'eau. . . .[6]

Her incredible confession to her husband, in which she confronts him with the tangible evidence that she has actually committed the crimes which he has dreamed of, is the story's central event. It is the moment in which the subterranean dialogue between the writer's rampant fascination with evil and her own obsession to take revenge on him for having sacrificed her to his "monsters" explodes into the open. The confession voices simultaneously her double's triumph and her authentic self's desperate plea to him to release her from the double's strangle hold by accepting his responsibility for its existence.

> Sais-tu qui je suis? Toutes celles, toutes celles que tu as rêvées, plus chères que des vivantes. . . . J'avais lu tes livres, moi! Je les ai poursuivies dans tes livres, avec quelle curiosité dévorante! Tu ne leur avais donné, avec tout ton génie, qu'une existence douteuse, une forme impalpable, légère, —je leur ai donné mieux; un corps, de vrais muscles, une volonté, un bras! . . . Oh! j'étais entre leurs mains comme dans les doigts du modeleur! Quel vertige! Quelle amère ivresse! . . . Ah! si on avait su! Ils n'avaient de ton oeuvre que le reflet, mais ils l'auraient vue en moi resplendir et se consumer![7]

[6] *Dialogues d'ombres*, pp. 11–12.
[7] *Ibid.*, p. 20.

In Madame Dargent's secret life which at last emerges to the surface, we find an early example of that alchemic heightening of vitality that results from the Bernanosian dialogue of shadows and that signifies not an authentic blossoming but a feverish reversal of the true self's quest for freedom and redemption into the double's blind return to chaos under the spell of the writer's evil dreams. In an apparently heightened state of determination and lucid will, whose source is pure delusion, Madame Dargent has pursued the "arid, cursed path" of his criminal heroines and acted out not her own destiny but the role dictated to her by the horror and despair he has aroused in her. While seeking with every fiber of her being to defend herself against his abortive creatures, she has succumbed to them to the point where her own revolt and their reckless adventures have become indistinguishable from one another.

> Que tu leur as prêté de vices [she says of his heroines]! Combien de crimes ingénieux dont vous avez ensemble caressé la pensée! Et qu'elles m'ont été fidèles! Car il est dur de marcher seule, dans la route aride et maudite! Mais à chaque obstacle, c'était l'une d'elles qui se levait en silence, droite, impérieuse, et me fixant d'un regard animal. . . . Rien ne pouvait plus m'arrêter. . . . Leur audace et mon audace croissait avec le danger. . . . Quelquefois je faiblissais, je tremblais, dans leurs mains si fermes. . . . Alors elles entraient en moi, elles agissaient pour moi. . . .[8]

We see the double's moves of vengeance entailing an ever-increasing sense of exile and self-violation. Each act in the execution of her role has left the heroine more drained of strength and closer to the final shipwreck. After she has violated herself beyond all measure—her agony anticipates Mouchette's "horrible spasm [in *Sous le Soleil de Satan*] of not just playing a role, but playing the role

[8] *Ibid.*, p. 22.

one loathes!"[9]—we see the dying heroine in the story's moment of crisis at last throttled by the double's grip. The seemingly limitless expanse of her *mensonges*, through which she has seen herself moving toward freedom purely on the strength of her own will and cunning, like a triumphant vehicle of destruction, reveals itself to be the snare set by "another," whose game she has been duped into playing and which she must break away from even at the cost of a sudden and complete foundering.

Dargent's only response to the "explosion" of her confession is abject terror:

> Il a la sensation de descendre au creux de la vague, au milieu d'une rumeur immense.[10]

Unable to arrest and tame the flood which he himself has conjured up, he is spellbound by its satanic mirror. With tragic irony, it holds up before him his justification by reflecting his own and his wife's roles in reverse:

> C'est elle, c'est elle, le mauvais ange, la diabolique Providence, son destin, son destin tragique![11]

In a symbolic response, he strangles her and thus reasserts the false creator's only power—the power to destroy.

In *Un Mauvais Rêve*, Bernanos has created a complete fictional evocation of the aborted creative act, specifically, an aborted novel. The reader is introduced into the laboratory in which Ganse, the master alchemist, is conducting his experiments, is led through preliminary exercises to the dramatic master experiment, and in the novel's final pages witnesses the ultimate violent explosion.

---

[9] *Sous le Soleil de Satan*, p. 69.
[10] *Dialogue d'ombres*, p. 24.
[11] *Ibid.*, p. 31.

A shadow of unreality, of "literature," is cast over the opening of the work. Through Olivier de Mainville's letter to his provincial aunt—Bernanos' ironic *pastiche* of a young Balzacian hero's letter home which, as we find out later, is not even Olivier's own effort, but Simone Alfieri's—we are introduced into a post-World-War-I Paris in which life and literature have become indistinguishable from one another. The two adolescents, Olivier, Ganse's orphaned assistant, and Philippe, the writer's "nephew"—he is actually the bastard son of one of Ganse's former mistresses—are bad pieces of literature. Both are pitifully self-conscious, declamatory, and out of touch with themselves and reality. The fraudulent city—suggesting a pale reflection of Balzac's inferno—in which they find themselves drifting has alienated them even further. Very quickly they have found themselves pushed into playing the role of disenchanted young men who revolt against the cynicism of the times by serving the cause of letters. This role holds two major advantages for their elders: first, it diverts into a seemingly innocuous channel the boys' real anxiety at finding themselves unwanted and superfluous in a "world of old men"; and second, it provides the *littérateurs*, who like everyone else are "at the end of their rope,"[12] with convenient and very malleable models for the always profitable subject of "modern youth."

"We never get out of literature."[13] Olivier's despairing remark to Simone Alfieri betrays his sense of alienation and imprisonment. To escape it, the boy has retreated into his own private phantasy, a Narcissus myth through which, in the absence of an authentic ideal or master, he has made himself the object of his own idolatrous admiration.

12 *Un Mauvais Rêve*, p. 78.
13 *Ibid.*, p. 156.

> . . . ses plaisirs à vingt ans restaient ceux de la délicate
> adolescence: la fierté de son jeune corps caressé sous la
> douche, les longues matinées paresseuses, débordantes
> d'une lassitude ineffable, le glissement au sommeil par des
> routes mystérieuses bordées de visages voluptueux. . . .[14]

Both he and Philippe are too young and innocent, however,
not to need a high priest for their artificial paradise. That
high priest turns out, of course, to be Ganse. The novelist's
sharp eye has no trouble discerning at a glance the pathetic
blight which is concealed underneath the boys' self-assured
airs and their readiness to worship anyone who will take
them seriously. He attaches them to himself by a display
of paternal interest, then begins to exploit them and their
myths shamelessly for literary material. Philippe, who has
preceded Olivier by some months in the novelist's intimacy,
pours out his wrath to the novice:

> Tenez, au début, ça bichait très bien entre nous, mon oncle
> et moi—à ne pas croire! . . . J'étais pour lui la jeunesse
> moderne, la jeunesse moderne, c'était moi. Et sans en avoir
> trop l'air—car il est rusé, au fond, le vieux singe!—sa grosse
> patte tachée d'encre me poussait tout doucement—toc!
> toc!—j'aurais fait la culbute dans un de ses livres. Le pis,
> voyez-vous, c'est que je serais devenu facilement l'un de ces
> quelconques guignols dont il croit tenir les ficelles, et qui
> sont tous, quoi qu'il en dise, d'abominables petits Ganse—je
> devenais Ganse. . . .[15]

For the aging Ganse, as for the anxiety-ridden, confes-
sion-seeking society whose prophet he has become, literature is no longer an art which freely shapes and evokes an
imaginative response to life. It has become a compulsive
act of invading the secrets of human beings and events and
of secretly venting through them his own phobias. Ganse,
who sees himself as another Balzac, a fountain of inexhaustible creative power, is or has become a Louis Lambert,

[14] *Ibid.*, p. 43.   [15] *Ibid.*, pp. 31–32.

condemned to exhaust himself in the futile effort to master life through the power of his will and intellect alone. In defiance of all his conscious efforts, each new character he creates is just one more reflection of his repressed fascination with evil and death. His subjects elude him simply because he is so trapped within himself that he is unable to focus his vision on anything outside himself. As the force of his will approaches the breaking point, his overworked brain loses more and more control of his material and falls prey to the monstrously proliferating fragments of all the aborted plots and characters which his imagination has failed to bring to life and which continue to ferment. Victim of the "ferocious irony" which characterizes the satanic, he sees this proliferation as a proof of his creative power:

> Par une ironie féroce, l'imagination surmenée ne cessait de multiplier, jusqu'à l'absurde, au cauchemar, ces créatures inachevées, mêlées à des lambeaux d'histoires, dont le grouillement donne au malheureux l'illusion, sans cesse renaissante, de la puissance qu'il a perdue.[16]

The more completely his imagination is choked off at its source by his unacknowledged fear of death and his insane ambition, the more merciless that curiosity becomes through which he seeks to compensate for its failure. Ganse's curiosity, like that of all the great Bernanosian antagonists, is closely related to the thirst of the satanic abyss. Unable to see, in the creative sense of bringing to light and giving insight into the subject's inner structure, Ganse is reduced to aping the creative process by concentrating his attention on the minutiae of the subject's exterior and on those fundamentally anonymous reflections of anxiety and self-hatred that testify only to the human soil's invasion by the satanic water. His wager to prove himself to be the Balzac of his generation and to "squash

[16] *Ibid.*, p. 101.

his publisher beneath him'"[17] turns his life into an agonizing hunt for subjects and a succession of endless journeys of documentation, in which he tracks down the minutest details of his locales and characters in the hope of coming up with a clue to their "secret lives."

> Le sujet! Son sujet [Olivier writes to his aunt in describing him]! Aujourd'hui même que sa curiosité survit à sa puissance, quand le regard dévore de loin ce que l'imagination affaiblie ne fécondera plus, que son effrayante besogne est devenue le drame des matins et des soirs, avec des alternations d'euphorie traîtresse, de rage, d'angoisse, ce mot de sujet semble n'éveiller en lui que l'idée de rapt et d'étreinte, il a l'air de vouloir refermer dessus ses grosses mains.[18]

But no subject appears able to draw out of the novelist the great work he dreams of. In the same reversal of roles which has already been encountered in the *Dialogue d'ombres*, Ganse blames the world for his own sterility. "It's not I who am empty . . . it's they," he says contemptuously of his contemporaries. "The world is emptying itself from below, like the dead. Nothing left in the belly, no more belly."[19] The young are the special objects of his rage. It is his ruthless betrayal of their faith in him that is destroying the two boys—Philippe commits suicide in the seventh chapter, thus realizing his announced

> . . . départ pour des régions inaccessibles à sa littérature, et où je ne risquerai plus, à chaque pas, de marcher sur un de ses crapauds bavards.[20]

and the panic-stricken Olivier succumbs to the fatal spell and morphine of Simone Alfieri. Yet Ganse sees himself as the betrayed one. In the satanic interplay of shadows, we see here another example of the most fatal of all reversals of images: the antagonist sees himself defrauded of his hope

[17] *Ibid.*   [18] *Ibid.*, p. 14.   [19] *Ibid.*, p. 74.
[20] *Ibid.*, p. 40.

for a "new childhood" by the young, while the children suffer the rape he inflicts on them in the form of guilt and shame. Ganse becomes venomous in his attack on Olivier. In the reflection of Olivier's pallid, vacuous ennui, his own ennui, or feverish thirst for life, becomes unbearable to him:

> Nous ne nous ennuierons jamais ensemble, comprenez-vous [he screams at him]? Votre ennui est stérile—un ennui limpide et fade, comme l'eau. . . .[21]

But if the boys prove too weak and unsubstantial to serve Ganse as a foil and deliver him from his obsession, his dreams are kindled to explosion by Simone Alfieri. The collaboration between Ganse and his mysterious secretary is painted as a strange and prolific "unnatural marriage" which has for a long time enabled him to maintain an illusion of creative plenitude.

The silent, strangely self-possessed Simone Alfieri, whose eyes have the "oblique glance of Leonardo's models,"[22] is an absorbing mystery to the novelist, which he cannot unravel. The widow of an Italian count and adventurer whose sudden death some years back caused rumors, never fully silenced, of murder, she represents to the plebeian Ganse the nobility and glamour he has hankered after all his life, with the added fascination of something untoward, something sensational in her past that excites the flair of the detective writer. An ambiguous radiance or mirror-like fluidity emanates from her. Its source we discover, is a total *disponibilité* which enables her to penetrate and draw out of her master his most reckless phantasies and to play some part in giving them shape. This *disponibilité*, which bears the closest resemblance to the selflessness of love, turns out to be its very opposite. It derives, not from the self-oblivion and subsequent freedom of response that is

[21] *Ibid.*, p. 63.   [22] *Ibid.*, p. 46.

characteristic of love, but from a violent self-repudiation that has been induced by injured pride. As the mystery of *Un Mauvais Rêve* unfolds, we see that Simone Alfieri's life is spellbound by an evil dream: she lives in the delusion that if she can dedicate herself to translating the dreams of others into reality, become their mirror and "providence," she will be released from the bonds of her past and hateful self, to enter the intoxicating paradise of limitless power. Only a vague aura of sadness distinguishes the evil dream or delusion of her life from the compelling radiance of the child's and the saint's vision of Paradise. It suggests that the source of her dream is not the limpid, azure spring of grace but the deep water of death.

Ganse is awed by the perverse heroism he senses in her, her "dazzling superiority." He grasps very well that her sacrificial dedication to his work, which is saving him from despair, has its source in the unquenchable ennui that has insinuated itself into her ardent dream of self-surpassing love and has "slowly poisoned, rotted, liquefied it":

> Un homme réellement supérieur [he explains to Olivier, whose insignificance remains unenhanced even by despair] est naturellement sacrificiel, il tend à s'immoler pour quelque objet qui le dépasse, il risque de devenir ce que nous appelons un héros ou un saint. Ça réussit une fois sur mille. Beaucoup d'appelés, hein? peu d'élus. Reste le vice. . . . J'ignore d'ailleurs ce qu'ils entendent par sainteté. Mais je ne suis pas éloigné de croire que Mme. Alfieri soit une espèce de sainte—oh! sans miracles, naturellement—une sainte triste. . . . Supposez qu'une sainteté ait quelque faille, quelque fissure par où se glisse l'ennui. . . . La sainteté peu à peu empoisonnée, pourrie, liquéfiée par l'ennui. . . .[23]

The satanic transmutation of Simone Alfieri's dream of Paradise into an evil dream has, so we learn, begun early in her life and has progressively turned her pursuit of the

[23] *Ibid.*, pp. 64, 65.

azure "land of fountains" into a movement of evasion and return. Significantly, she describes its first major phase, her marriage with Alfieri, as a rapturous flight into an exotic Baudelairian paradise,

> . . . dans le vertige de la vanité comblée, des hauts et enflammés délires d'orgueil.[24]

> Tu n'imagines pas [she tells Olivier], ces soleils, ces palais qui trempent dans l'eau bleue, et ces odeurs. . . . Oh! je sais bien, les nigauds prétendent rêver de grands voyages solitaires. Ils ne comprennent rien à cette découverte flamboyante, projetée d'Océan en Océan.[25]

The flight ended abruptly in "the void, in nothingness."[26] Instead of setting her free, the exploits and caprices of the dissolute Alfieri drew her ever more deeply into the "thirsty water." Working at every turn upon her lacerated pride and blocking from her sight any positive challenge worthy of her passion, his phantasies exacerbated her to a point of frenzy:

> Avec celui-là, pas moyen de rester en repos—si faible, si lâche, si fille, si vraiment fille!—avec un tel besoin du vice d'autrui, comme s'il n'eût pu goûter le mal qu'à travers une âme étrangère. Lorsqu'il vous coulait un certain regard, on avait envie de lui mettre un crime dans la main. Un crime, un beau crime. . . .[27]

When she first meets Ganse and accepts the chance to work with him, it is with the secret hope that he will free her of the nightmares that are closing in on her. The novelist represents to her tormented soul a creative force that will release her true strength and, by freeing her from the mesmerizing eye of the sea, restore her lost sense of direction.

---

[24] *Ibid.*, p. 157.   [25] *Ibid.*, pp. 156–57.   [26] *Ibid.*, p. 82.
[27] *Ibid.*, p. 82.

But Ganse's notice is immediately drawn to her flooded inner life (though it is carefully concealed), which promises to provide a fertile hunting ground for his increasingly more sterile imagination. Instead of opening her eyes to the world and to the immense drama of death and redemption in which she has a part to play, he tracks down and plays with fiendish complicity on her unconscious despair. She is forced to recognize in his writings her most destructive impulses, potentiated by the power of his own "thirst." She in turn, as her desire to serve him becomes engulfed in her need to defy him and avenge herself, begins to exasperate him by calmly holding up to him the daily evidence of his waning productivity. Gradually, the exchange and inter-action of the most destructive longings and phantasies of both take on the form of a deadly duel, in which each is simultaneously the other's jailor and prisoner and seeks to conjure the other's "evil dream" in order to exorcise his own. As her strength matches his, their mutual fascination and hatred keeps growing. For a time it produces a pro-liferation of dubious, aborted works. Ganse, willfully blind both to the sterility and to the potential destructiveness of their "alchemy of dreams," particularly for her who does not, like himself, have a safety valve in writing, relishes it as a sure means of continued productivity:

> Pourquoi n'échangerait-on pas des rêves et surtout des mauvais rêves, les mauvais rêves sont lourds . . . les rêves, ça se combine ou ça ne se combine pas—une vraie chimie. Quand la proportion y est —pfutt![28]

The fatal explosion becomes imminent when Ganse at last conceives the idea of turning Simone Alfieri herself into the subject of a novel. He is convinced that, having his heroine daily before his eyes, he will have no trouble what-ever in carrying off this work with dispatch. Through this

[28] *Ibid.*, p. 67.

last gross violation, however, he turns his collaborator into a bitter and vengeful enemy who is determined to defend his subject's secret from Ganse's deadly "thirst." All his cajoling, probing and threatening fail utterly to draw out of her the coveted mystery of her past. His eye fastens on every detail of her features, every expression, every gesture that might give him the clue he needs to work out his fictional Evangéline's fate, but to no avail. Simone's infinitely resourceful pride counters and rebuffs his most cunning invasions into her private life. "You have the pride of a demon," he concedes with grim admiration.

> Parlez-moi de diables tranquilles, de braves types de diables, des diables pourceaux. A vous, ma petite, il vous faut le serpent.[29]

The sight of Simone Alfieri—whose real name, we learn, is the same as his heroine's, Evangéline—furnishes only the intolerable mirror in which he is forced finally to acknowledge his impotence.

Upon his failure to deliver himself of the phantasy which she has aroused, by mastering it and bringing his *Evangéline* to a *dénouement*, Ganse appears to evaporate, much like Ouine, into nothingness. He simply vanishes from the novel; but not until Simone Alfieri has overwhelmed him with the full satanic impact of his evil dreams on her life and their approaching explosion into reality. The phantasmagoria of which for years he has relieved himself by foisting them on her has taken over her inner life so completely that nothing sound is left in her.

> Vous m'avez remplie de vos créatures, j'étouffe. Oui, j'étouffe réellement. Que je tarde encore à redevenir moi-même, et je ne pourrai jamais plus.[30]

---

[29] *Ibid.*, p. 84.   [30] *Ibid.*, pp. 82–83.

She announces that she is leaving him in order to save herself from the demons he has conjured up and to "become herself again." But she is deluding herself: even in leaving Ganse, she carries within her the incubus of his satanic heroine and must be delivered of her. In a state of lucid delirium, Simone Alfieri, like Madame Dargent, sees her double emerging out of the depths of the sea—here, Ganse's "thirsty" glance—and mistakes it for her own self:

> C'est étonnant de voir ainsi monter peu à peu son propre visage dans le miroir que vous tendez, on a l'impression de se regarder à travers une grande épaisseur d'eau trouble, avec des bulles de boue.[31]

In a passage which bears a close resemblance to the climax of Madame Dargent's confession, the now live embodiment of his Evangéline confronts the horror-stricken Ganse with the murder she is about to commit and which will "complete his book."[32] This murder turns out to be the end product of their "alchemy of evil dreams," the explosive act through which, ironically, the violated subject will, under the impact of an intoxicating dream of defiance and revenge, seek to free herself from him by acting out the very role he has created for her.

In the phantasmagoric second part of *Un Mauvais Rêve*, the towering presence of the master is superseded by that of the subject, who now surpasses his most reckless dreams. The figure of Simone Alfieri assumes the dimensions of an evil Angel, a supernatural power which nothing can check. Her journey to Souville to kill Olivier's aunt and thus bring the boy into possession of a large fortune represents the victory of "literature," in its unredeemed aspect of an unmastered, boundless thirst for life, over life, or of an evil dream over reality.

[31] *Ibid.*, p. 88.   [32] *Ibid.*

Peut-être est-il plus ou moins sorti de la littérature [she says of the crime], mais nulle force ne le contraindrait d'y rentrer.[33]

Bernanos' evocation of the journey is a masterpiece and certainly the best part of the novel. It is conceived as a slow, inevitable surrender to the depths of delusion. We see Simone Alfieri propelled towards the crime as a sleepwalker to the precipice, by a force over which she has no control. In the reversed vision which is characteristic of the satanic shadow or double, she sees the murder she is about to commit as an act of free, unbounded will, as a providential act that will assert her own unlimited power over life and assure the happiness of her subject, Olivier.

Until the actual explosion of her evil dream into reality takes place, the solid obstacles and piercing sounds of reality that puncture the gliding movement and dreamlike silence of her journey seem indeed powerless to awaken her. The entire journey is presented as a battle between the deep, treacherous ocean of delusion whose captive she has become and the harsh soil of reality, in which the fluid element easily retains the upper hand. We see the infallible logic of her delirium dictate her every move from the moment she boards the train. Its smoothness is reenforced by the effect of a shot of morphine, her "favorite poison." As she sits in her compartment, her mind riveted on the old lady whose image has been obsessing her and whose fate she now holds in her hands, she is engulfed in a deep euphoria of power.

But soon, reality begins to intrude, in the form of "a stupid enemy, the stupidest of all, chance."[34] At first it is nothing more than the shrill whistle of a locomotive which gives her an anguished start:

[33] *Ibid.*, p. 90.   [34] *Ibid.*, p. 191.

> Le sifflet d'une locomotive en manoeuvre déchirait l'air
> de son appel funèbre, parfois prolongé comme une plainte,
> parfois bref, impérieux, désespéré, pareil au cri d'un être
> conscient, frappé de mort.[35]

The battle gains momentum as the journey approaches its
conclusion. She gropes her way through the darkness on a
borrowed bicycle, and the forest's narrow, labyrinthine
paths become more and more arduous to follow. She grows
weary and anxious. A new dose of the peace-dispensing drug
shuts out once more the threatening warning signals. It
enfolds her in a dream in which time and space are dissolved and she sees the murder as a thing of a distant,
long-forgotten past:

> Il lui semble que la maison grise recule à une vitesse verti-
> gineuse, s'enfonce. Dieu! est-il vrai que la chose est faite,
> accomplie, oubliée . . . comme la nuit est noire, noire et
> douce![36]

Again, reality counters with a stunning blow. Suddenly,
in the middle of the forest, a young priest who has lost his
way emerges right before her eyes, and she is forced for a
while to walk along the path by his side. His youth and his
simple, plain words cause her an extraordinary agitation.
As he talks to her about himself and looks at her trustfully,
something like a deeply buried memory begins to stir in her
and floods her with sudden pain. It is her own submerged
self, to which he is spontaneously appealing.

> 'Où l'ai-je vu?' se demandait-elle sans conviction, mais avec
> le vague espoir que sa mémoire finirait par répondre à
> l'appel, fournirait une explication plausible, non à cette
> rencontre bizarre mais au trouble qui l'agitait.[37]

Still, her immunity, safeguarded by the morphine, prevails. She is shaken by the encounter but, summoning her

[35] *Ibid.*, p. 199.   [36] *Ibid.*, p. 218.   [37] *Ibid.*, p. 224.

courage, manages to leave her companion abruptly and continues on her solitary pursuit. It turns into a nightmare. She overshoots her mark and comes out on a steep path that she cannot negotiate on the bicycle. She dismounts. Pushing the heavy bicycle up the slippery path soon exhausts her strength. Once again, the effect of the morphine is wearing off, and as her fatigue and lucidity keep increasing, so does her awareness of the danger and hopelessness of the course into which she has been drawn:

> La route étroite luisait à ses pieds. . . . A ce moment, dégrisée par la peur, l'absurdité de son entreprise, la certitude de son échec lui apparurent de nouveau avec une telle force d'évidence qu'elle ferma les yeux comme sous un choc en pleine poitrine, étouffa un gémissement. Le désespoir seul avait pu l'amener jusque-là—un désespoir dont elle n'avait jamais eu qu'à de rares minutes, une claire conscience— désespoir sans cause et sans objet précis, d'autant plus redoutable qu'il s'était lentement infiltré en elle, imprégnant ainsi qu'un autre poison plus subtil chaque fibre de sa chair, courant à travers ses veines avec son sang. Nulle parole n'eût pu l'exprimer, nulle image lui donner assez de réalité pour frapper son intelligence, tirer sa volonté de son engourdissement stupide. A peine se souvenait-elle de l'enchaînement des circonstances, liées entre elles par la logique délirante du rêve, qui l'avaient entraînée jusque-là, et pour quel dessein elle était venue. . . .[38]

Unable to extricate herself from the "insane logic of her dream," she is carried by it to the horrible final goal in which at last it takes on a tangible form. The murder of the old lady takes place with the swiftness and soundlessness of a nightmare, and with the now ironic complicity of chance. But instantaneously, we see its explosive force blast open the closed world of shadows. The act not only kills Olivier's aunt but it wipes out, in the same decisive

[38] *Ibid.*, pp. 233–34.

blow, the overwhelming shadow or double that has usurped Simone Alfieri's inner life and turned it into a "flood of *mensonges*."[39] The moment the murder is accomplished, she finds herself infinitely removed from it: it is not her act, but the act of "another." She herself is face to face with the nothingness of pure despair. Everything about the satanic dream that she and Ganse have created together reveals itself to be a *mensonge*—the pretexts, the promises, the act itself, except for one thing: its deepest source, which the explosion has laid bare:

> La seule haine qu'elle eût vraiment connue, éprouvée, consommée jusqu'à la lie, c'était la haine de soi. Comme tout cela était clair! Pourquoi s'en avisait-elle si tard?[40]

In the final pages of *Un Mauvais Rêve*, Bernanos' deeply Christian imagination evokes, far more clearly than in the earlier *Madame Dargent*, the dynamic and potentially redemptive character of the fully realized, embodied event or act. Even, or maybe particularly, at its most destructive, it constitutes a crisis in which the hidden spiritual impetus or source is tested and forced to define itself. Every act, in the novelist's mature works, shares something of the efficacy of the mystery of the Incarnation. In the process of translating their evil dream into reality, his great antagonists are, unknown to themselves, drawn closer and closer to the ultimate moment of truth. At last, their *mensonge* or delusion of creative plenitude bursts like a bubble and they are forced to see themselves in their own nothingness. The very solidity and resistance of the concrete world becomes, in the Bernanosian drama of redemption, the natural weapon that divine grace employs to overcome the boundless delusions of satanic "thirst." Thus each crisis opens up the possibility that, when faced by the naked abyss of the

[39] *Ibid.*, p. 199.   [40] *Ibid.*, p. 243.

"thirsty water," the victim of the satanic dream may recoil
from it and let himself be saved by the love that has sought
to guide him all along.

The end of *Un Mauvais Rêve* leaves Simone Alfieri's fate
unresolved. Although her instinct of survival has prompted
her to avail herself of the almost miraculous chance to
escape unseen from the scene of the murder, the path she
has pursued under the dictate of Ganse's phantom has
come to a dead end. At that crucial moment, when one
further step would mean surrender to the abyss, she sees,
by a second incredible chance, the same young priest standing before her on the same path in the forest. This time she
no longer fails to recognize the challenge of his presence: it
is a silent but ardent invitation to tear her glance away
from the infinite, grandiose reflections of the sea and turn
it towards earth.

> Nul mensonge ne lui vint aux lèvres, et d'ailleurs, elle eût
> jugé vain n'importe quel mensonge. Ce prêtre fantastique,
> surgi deux fois des ténèbres, savait tout. Une seule chance
> lui restait peut-être, reconnaître sa funèbre puissance,
> s'avouer vaincue. . . .[41]

There the novel ends. Has the overwhelming shock of facing
the abyss purged Simone Alfieri's long-submerged dream of
love of its double, the dream of death? Will she entrust
herself to this witness of love who "knows everything"; or
will she confirm herself in her self-hatred by killing him,
and then herself? The curious alternate version of *Un
Mauvais Rêve*, and Bernanos' only attempt at a mystery
novel, which he produced as something of a *tour de force* in
1934, before casting *Un Mauvais Rêve* in its final form,
presents the more tragic of these two possibilities.

Despite its failure as a novel—it is not fully successful as
a mystery, nor does it really develop its stunning basic

[41] *Ibid.*, p. 253.

theme—*Un Crime* is a fascinating work, for it revolves around the most enigmatic aspect of the Bernanosian *mensonge*: the antagonist's thirst for the prophetic, life-giving role of the priest. More even than the "secret" of childhood, which in most lives does not survive the actual age of childhood,[42] it is the mystery of the "child of grace" that obsesses the novelist's sterile and avid usurpers of life. In first killing, then impersonating the new curé of Mégère, the heroine of *Un Crime* enacts, for the brief duration of her phantastic exploit, not only her mother's nostalgia for a lost Paradise but the evil dream of all the impostors who, inspired by a raging envy, seek to parody the priest's deep and vital communion with the mystery of creation through love, and presume to shape and direct human destinies. This dream motivates more or less distinctly the destinies of Ouine, Ganse, Simone Alfieri, the psychiatrists La Pérouse and Lipotte, and the great Cénabre, Bernanos' master impostor. It betrays all of them as "bad" priests. And the act it engenders in *Un Crime* is the purest of all distillations of evil. First, Evangéline murders the young priest. Then, in the characteristic manner of the satanic double, she usurps his mission and transforms it into a vehicle of blind rage. The toll of this rage is formidable: in addition to the two murders committed directly by the heroine and false curé, it takes three suicides—Evangéline's mother's, the boy André's, and finally her own—before its explosive force is finally spent.

The dialogue of shadows in which the satanic force of *Un Crime* has slowly gathered momentum before we see it breaking loose is of a more secret nature than that of either *Madame Dargent* or *Un Mauvais Rêve*. Its source is in Mme. Louise's fall—the love affair which, in the long distant past, forced the nun to abandon the religious life. Suppressed and

---

[42] *Dialogues des Carmélites*, p. 42.

unrepented, it has festered in her soul and turned her vocation into an obsession of nostalgia and guilt. This obsession she has unconsciously transmitted to her child. Evangéline's satanic delusion, in which she sees herself first as her friend's angel of providence, then as the priest of Mégère, is nothing but the potentiated reflection of her mother's obsession; and the grandiose adventure in which she kills the *châtelaine* whose heir the girl will be and the young priest on whom she stumbles in the forest, its unconscious enactment.

The little judge's intuition offers us a first and much needed clue to the deep link between the two shadowy and apparently unrelated figures of the possessed mother and daughter, which gives *Un Crime* its *raison d'être*:

> . . . j'ai acquis la conviction d'un secret commun au curé de Mégère et à . . . à cette dame Louise. . . .[43]

It also reconfirms the potential explosiveness of the Bernanosian evil dream by tracking the chain reaction that has led directly from the former nun's dissimulation and repression of the crucial episode to the gradual transformation of her whole inner life into an endlessly fermenting *mensonge*, and finally, to the false curé's sensational crime:

> . . . qu'elle ait pu dissimuler trente ans, voilà ce qui met en garde, mon cher. Je ne parle pas de mensonges: le menteur habituel est un escroc né, rien de plus—trop instable pour les vrais risques. La fidélité à un seul mensonge est un signe bien autrement grave. Une longue dissimulation doit faire éclore un jour ou l'autre le drame que chacun porte en soi, à son insu. La dissimulation couve le crime. . . .[44]

The figure of Evangéline, alias the curé of Mégère, differs from that of Simone Alfieri only by being more

---

[43] *Un Crime*, p. 194. [44] *Ibid.*, p. 195.

purely evil. Whereas in the heroine of *Un Mauvais Rêve* the dream of Paradise, of finding redemption by dedication to a creative force compelling enough to silence her demons, can be seen vying through the better part of the novel with her evil dream, the Evangéline of *Un Crime* is an almost pure incarnation of the Bernanosian *mensonge*. This may be owing in part to her being more sketchily drawn and not motivated until the very end of the novel. What we see of her before then is nothing but shadow and magical radiance, to which everyone who encounters her succumbs instantly. But even within the limited framework of a *roman policier*, her impersonation of the young priest whom she has murdered is evoked masterfully in its double aspect of delusion and reality. It is seen both as a triumphant assertion of freedom and, simultaneously, as the "impossible moment" of suspension that separates a vessel's explosion under the force of too great a pressure from its sinking out of sight.

At the end of the novel, when the explosion of her mother's and her own evil dream has finally fractured the heroine's double, an empty and hounded creature emerges at the surface for a moment, only to vanish again in the depths. Evangéline's suicide, which follows swiftly on the heels of her two murders and her mother's suicide, is the ultimate move in the return to nothingness on which her parent's secret thirst for self-destruction first launched her.

IV.

The Rock of Prometheus

Bernanos' great drama of a counterfeit priestly vocation is found in *L'Imposture* and *La Joie*, the two novels which the writer deplored not having the time to recast into one and which really form an indivisible whole. Here again, his powerful imagination displays the two fundamental forces which he saw underlying human existence and battling for possession of the human world: the roaring sea, rising up from the abyss of satanic hatred or "thirst," and, tender yet irresistible, the life-giving spring of divine love. But in these two early works, the central figure and pawn in the duel of the two waters is conceived in the image of an impenetrable rock.

Unlike the fluid, shadowy Ouine, or Simone Alfieri, or the false curé of Mégère, whose natural propensity inclines them to dream and who are basically creatures of water and easy victims of the enticing reflections of the satanic abyss, the virile figure of the Abbé Cénabre appears to have no affinity for water whatever. In contrast to the dreamers' journey of evasion, which starts as a narcissistic paradise, a euphoric surrender to the lure of their own image, Cénabre's path is from the very outset of his life the "arid road" of an iron self-discipline. From his earliest youth,

71

when the orphaned and poor peasant boy turned his back on the world in an unconscious movement of rebellion and decided to trust nothing but his own intellect and will, the hero of *L'Imposture* has sealed off his inner life tightly both from all outside currents and from its own deepest springs of faith and hope. The irony of his life is that while he has labored with painstaking tenacity to carry out the minutest obligations of his priestly life, he has kept his soul closed to the only true source which could sustain his vocation and make it fruitful: the love of God.

> Comment ne fut-il pas tenté d'aller plus loin, d'accorder à Dieu quelque chose de plus—un seul acte d'amour, au moins de bonne volonté—lorsque le champ remué n'attendait plus que la semence, un seul grain! Il est vrai que sa nature est d'une étonnante sécheresse. . . .[1]

Cénabre is Bernanos' most Promethean figure. As *L'Imposture,* and his impending crisis, begin, he is seen as a man of cold, hard self-possession, who has become so immured within himself that he can no longer either receive or impart the elements of life—the insight, hope, and strength which spring up everywhere and in the most unforeseeable contingencies for the soul grounded in love. For years, his massive resistance to the unsettling undercurrents of life has allowed him to live in the delusion that the superstructure of pure intellect and will which he has built for himself is safe against any assault, that his life can be a model of sanctity, "as if charity did not exist."[2]

> Etrange erreur d'un homme qui ne savait point encore que l'orgueil n'a rien en propre, n'est que le nom donné à l'âme qui se dévore elle-même.[3]

---

[1] *L'Imposture*, pp. 80–81.
[2] *Ibid.*, p. 29.
[3] *Ibid.*, p. 199.

Cénabre's barrenness represents, in the profound perspective of Bernanos' spiritual realism, the "impossible wager" of a human—and nothing but human—will, grounded in pride, which seeks to divorce itself from its supernatural source and assert its own autonomy. Of all evasions of reality, this is not only the most complete but in its very magnitude it represents the greatest offense and challenge to both the satanic and the divine powers thus defied. The very might of Cénabre's presumption, which has led him into the most sacred of all vocations in the confidence that he can daily confront with impunity the blood of the crucified God, marks Cénabre for tragedy. His role is unlike that of an Ouine or a Ganse. In his rigid autonomy he is not an antagonist who passively reflects as they do the satanic abyss and becomes a destroyer of others. Nor, obviously, is he a protagonist who can "lead mankind's march toward the Kingdom." The figure of the renegade priest is conceived as a chessman for whom we see both God and the Devil vying in a struggle to the death on a battleground which is his own tortured life.

In the dramatic development of his tragedy, which unfolds in five parts and reaches its climax on the last page of *La Joie*, the imagery which depicts the duel is of a petrified soil assaulted by two sources of water. The first of these is the polluted depth of Cénabre's own unconscious. Ironically, the superstructure designed to shield him from the assault of the sea has left his inner being defenseless against the deep "thirsty" water which roars below, ever active in its secret assault on the earth. From the poisoned spring of hope, a fermenting anxiety begins to well up. At first, it is nothing more than a sense of weariness and solitude. Gradually, however, like a hemmed-in flood, the anxiety gathers momentum and keeps rising, until it finally breaks through the surface. As "he sweats it through all his pores,"

he is stunned to recognize that the mainspring of his life
has turned into "pure, essential hatred."

> Il en était à cet excès d'angoisse où tout lien se trouve
> relâché, lorsque le corps participe, dans son ignominieuse
> détresse, au désastre même de l'âme . . . qu'il la sue par tous
> les pores. . . . Alors le mal se dénonce lui-même, s'avoue tel
> quel, non pas un mode de vivre, mais un attentat contre
> la vie.
> Ainsi cette fureur de haine . . . jaillissait enfin tout à fait
> hors du sanctuaire de la conscience. . . . C'était une haine
> impersonnelle, un jet de haine pure, essentielle.[4]

We see him defending himself against this surging tide with
the strength of a lion, stiffening himself against it at each
renewed assault, and reenforcing the heavy floodgates of
his reason and self-discipline until he has subdued it. But
the price to be paid for his victories is the slow asphyxiation
of his being and his transformation into a figure of living
death.

But early in the drama, another, equally mysterious
force begins to assail him, whose effect on him is the very
opposite. It is the fountain of living water or grace, which
will bear down on him through two of its most fragile and
defenseless, and yet all-powerful, vessels: first, the Abbé
Chevance, and then, after the latter's death, his spiritual
daughter Chantal de Clergerie. The influx of their tender,
glowing compassion is something which Cénabre's will resists in vain. Against all his efforts, it tends to loosen and
penetrate the rigid armor which is suffocating him. As the
poisons of self-hatred escape into the open, we see the
purified springs of his being produce the saving tears of
pity—pity for his own suffering and for the suffering of all
men—that flow directly from the infinite source of God's
own compassion:

[4] *Ibid.*, pp. 93–94.

. . . suprême invention de la miséricorde, universelle rançon . . . ce don sacré des larmes, ainsi qu'une nouvelle enfance![5]

In this double work, Bernanos evokes fully and explicitly what in the works discussed so far in this essay is only suggested—the formidable efficacy of God's own irony. From the outset of Cénabre's tragic story, we see the satanic irony of hatred which substitutes death for life, shadow for substance, challenged by the divine irony of love.

With the unlimited resourcefulness of its creative genius, we see love availing itself of every situation and contingency of Cénabre's life in order, first, to reveal to him the true distance which separates him from his goal of perfection and, simultaneously, to impel him to set his course straight in its pursuit. So dynamic does man's aspiration to freedom and wholeness of being reveal itself to be in the tragic destiny of this renegade priest, so powerful the impact, despite himself, of his long-repressed, long-forgotten dream of Paradise, that every step he takes that removes him further from his true goal unleashes more anguish, until at last anguish awakens him from his delusion.

In the dynamic and ever-shifting Bernanosian drama, in which nothing less than the human world's salvation is at stake at every moment, we discover not only the deep links which bind together his humanity in a common quest for the Kingdom of the Father's love but, more interestingly, the constant interaction within the hero's own being of spirit and flesh, water and earth. As the great Bernanosian delusions or *mensonges* are invariably aberrations of the spirit, reflecting the Fallen Angel's thirst for power over life, we see in *L'Imposture* and *La Joie* the hero's finite, earthly body pay the penalty and, through its suffering,

[5] *Ibid.*, p. 101.

become the instrument of his redemption. It is the body, crucified by anguish, which testifies to the soul's violation and wrenches it out of its delusion. In the extremity of Cénabre's "shipwreck" or hopeless physical disarray, in which the false self-image is fractured, love itself is at work. Not allowing the victim's inner being to be drowned in the flood of satanic hatred without warning, it will patiently lead him to the crisis where anguish will use any opening, albeit the deadliest explosion at the end of his "cursed road," to rid his being of its poisons:

> . . . si subtil que soit l'ennemi, sa plus ingénieuse malice ne saurait atteindre l'âme que par un détour, ainsi qu'on force une ville en empoisonnant ses sources. Il trompe le jugement, souille l'imagination, émeut la chair et le sang, use avec un art infini de nos propres contradictions, égare nos joies, approfondit nos tristesses, fausse les actes et les intentions dans leurs rapports secrets, mais quand il a ainsi tout bouleversé, il n'a encore rien détruit. C'est de nous qu'il lui faut tirer le suprême consentement, et il ne l'aura point que Dieu n'ait parlé à son tour, Si longtemps qu'il ait cru retarder la grâce divine, elle doit jaillir, et il en attend le jaillissement nécessaire, inéluctable dans une terreur immense, car son patient travail peut être détruit en un instant. . . .[6]

In Bernanos' Christian and hence tragic vision, the Serpent's irony does indeed triumph in the realm of time by claiming a fearful toll in arrested and shipwrecked human existences. But in the ultimate dimension of the drama of man's quest for Paradise, which transcends the natural boundaries of life and death and in which life means the soul's facing God and death its return to nothingness, the satanic victory is by no means assured. At the end of *La Joie*, Cénabre's breakdown, which marks the end for him from a purely earthbound point of view, is seen as the

[6] *Ibid.*, p. 103.

possible beginning of his redemption. It is that mysterious moment of conversion when the irresistible outpouring by Chantal of "the divine hope which was the source of her life"[7] has at last purged his vision of perfection of its deceitful shadow and left him face to face with the Father.

In the opening part of *L'Imposture*, which has the explosive character of the first act of a tragedy, the two forces that have been contending for Cénabre's life in secret break into the open. Time is foreshortened in this chapter. It takes less than a day for the until then profoundly calm and self-contained priest to be shaken by the first nearly fatal assault of the deadly water of satanic hatred and, almost simultaneously, by the to him even more terrible assault of the heavenly water of mercy. Already, while engrossed in writing a study on the Florentine mystics, he has had the humiliating experience of realizing that in each saint whom his avid intelligence has sought to analyze an essential mystery has eluded him. All have turned out to be mere hollow reflections of himself, taunting him with the evidence of his own spiritual barrenness.

> C'est que de la vérité violentée, comme l'odeur dénonce un cadavre, à travers les mots menteurs, sourd une ironie atroce . . . dont l'abbé Cénabre connaît la morsure. Anxieux de se fuir, d'ailleurs épris de ces personnages imaginaires qu'il substitue presque inconsciemment aux vrais, qu'il s'efforce de rendre vrais . . . il ne rencontre que lui, toujours lui. . . . Il se voit nu.[8]

Here we find the first and familiar Bernanosian manifestation of satanic thirst—the still unconscious need to feed on the living inner spring of the "children of grace" through intellectual penetration, and a subsequently intensified sense of barrenness.

---

[7] *La Joie*, p. 37.   [8] *L'Imposture*, p. 31.

In the opening episode, this carefully repressed sensation bursts into Cénabre's consciousness, and with it a piercing awareness that his entire priestly life has been a *mensonge*, that it is founded on nothing but delusion. The incident that calls forth the crisis is in itself minor: Pernichon, a vain little diocesan journalist whose spiritual director Cénabre has been for some time, is in the priest's study. Suddenly Cénabre finds himself yielding to an irresistible impulse to demolish him. In Pernichon's "effeminate soul, his muddy, ambiguous, never-aired, unhealthy inner life,"[9] Cénabre has glimpsed a reflection of something too loathsome for him to face. In a rage never before experienced he crushes his defenseless penitent with the words, "Your inner life, my child, bears the sign minus,"[10] and dismisses him. After Pernichon has gone, the outwardly majestically calm priest finds himself unable, to his astonishment, to collect himself. The rage which has broken out of him so unexpectedly submerges him like a sweeping tide, threatening to leave nothing intact of the fraudulent structure that he has taken to be his life and vocation:

> Par un suprême effort, les arguments familiers surgissent de toutes parts, dans un désordre affreux. Mais il sent trop, il sent avec terreur que cette confusion n'est qu'un remous, à la surface d'une eau profonde. Déjà la pensée, l'unique, la précieuse, la dangereuse pensée jaillie de lui est descendue bien plus avant, hors de toute atteinte, glisse à travers les ténèbres ainsi que le poids d'une sonde. Elle ne s'arrêtera qu'au but, s'il existe. L'homme suspendu par ses mains défaillantes, à demi ouvertes, au-dessus du gouffre, n'écoute pas avec plus d'angoisse la chute vaine et bondissante des pierres.[11]

By an effect of divine irony, the *mensonge* of the Abbé Cénabre's vocation is brought out into the open, into the field of his consciousness, by the very triumph of the satanic

[9] *Ibid.*, p. 9.   [10] *Ibid.*, p. 16.   [11] *Ibid.*, pp. 34–35.

water. It is through the rent it has torn in his armor that
he catches the first glimpse of the gaping void on which he
has tried to build his own perfection. The shock of the
discovery stuns him.

> A la lettre, il ne sentait ni regret ni remords. Seul, l'étonne-
> ment d'un homme qui, croyant marcher dans une direction,
> connaîtrait qu'il a piétiné, que l'espace franchi n'est qu'un
> rêve. . . . Par la brèche mystérieuse, le passé tout entier
> avait glissé comme une eau, et il ne demeurait, sous le
> regard inaltérable de la conscience, que des gestes plus
> vains que des songes, une vie ordonnée, réglée, constituée
> en fonction d'un monde imaginaire.[12]

The abrupt termination of that phase of his "path of
evasion" in which he was still a blind victim of his own
pride, sustained by the flawlessness of his *mensonge*, now
confronts him with an agonizing alternative: he must either
attempt to bury as quickly as possible the crushing knowledge of his life's falseness and barrenness and continue on
the road "on which no rest is possible" because each day's
work, as soon as it is done, is dissolved again like a mirage,
or he must surrender instantly to the gulf that has opened
up beneath him. For a moment, the temptation to do the
latter is irresistible. In a to him new state of satanic
rapture, Cénabre lets himself sink. However, what awaits
him is not peace but the deep, hidden spring of self-hatred
which has been poisoning him.

> Bien qu'il s'abandonnât désormais, cet abandon ne lui
> apportait aucun soulagement certain: une issue semblait
> ouverte, au contraire, aux eaux dormantes et pourries
> de l'âme. Des sentiments nouveaux, et pourtant familiers
> à sa nature profonde, impossibles à renier, sourdaient
> ensemble d'un sol saturé. A sa grande surprise, le plus fort
> d'entre eux ressemblait singulièrement à la haine.[13]

[12] *Ibid.*, pp. 35–36.   [13] *Ibid.*, p. 38.

His anguish becomes so intense that, "like a man shouting on the edge of the sea,"[14] he blindly reaches for help. He needs someone to whom he can cling; someone on whom he can unburden himself of his terror without having to face up to its true source; someone whom he can convince, thereby convincing himself, that he has merely undergone one of those moments of barrenness and temptation to which all religious souls are subject. But once again this new lie, which is designed to stop up and return to oblivion the terrible secret of his spiritual non-existence, explodes right in his face. Ironically, the "witness" whom Cénabre summons in the dead of night, because he considers the man a deferential simpleton who would not dare question him, is one of God's elect, who sees "with the eyes of an angel."[15]

In his own person a timorous, awkward little man whose insignificance contrasts strikingly with Cénabre's imposing figure and bearing, the Abbé Chevance is, in the root of his being, a transparent vessel of grace. Possessing nothing in his own name, indeed incapable of possessing or holding anything, his whole existence is dedicated not to consolidating his self but to letting it flow out freely to whatever soul his loving eye shows him to be in need of cleansing and quickening. In contrast to the "thirsty" water we see rising up within the Abbé Cénabre's being, seeking to steal and hoard life, Chevance's secret is the ineffable and inexhaustible spring of divine love that flows through him and spends itself in a ceaseless gift of life to others. His life and this spring are one,

> . . . la miséricorde divine dont il était plein . . . confondue à l'effusion de sa propre vie. . . .[16]

[14] *Ibid.*, p. 53.   [15] *Ibid.*, p. 55.   [16] *Ibid.*, p. 50.

In contrast to the eye of the victim of delusion, which blindly reflects the thirst of the abyss, the limpid glance of the Abbé Chevance, as he gazes at Cénabre and listens to him, reflects with overwhelming power the latter's true state of spiritual asphyxiation. Unable to believe for a moment the story of Cénabre's doubt and despair, Chevance not only does not help his confrere to disguise the source of his anguish but forces him to see it more clearly than before. In a renewed upsurge of rage, Cénabre strikes him but is overcome immediately by a strange, vibrant feeling of true shame:

> Il restait muet devant sa grotesque victime, la discernant à peine, toute son attention tendue vers l'événement intérieur, le jaillissement irrésistible, la force inconnue, surnaturelle. . . . Qu'était, qu'était cette passion soudaine, frappant de tels coups dans sa poitrine?[17]

The Abbé Chevance begs Cénabre to relinquish the pretenses and the self-deception which are poisoning his life at its source, or at least, if he can do no more, to repudiate them in his heart:

> Il voyait, il tenait sous son regard, il touchait presque l'âme forcenée, frappée à mort; il n'espérait plus rien d'elle qu'un signe, qu'un seul signe, à peine volontaire, à peine lucide, quelque chose comme le clin d'oeil qui consent, sur la face pétrifiée de l'agonie, un rien, la brêche où put peser de tout son poids immense la formidable pitié divine, qu'il entendait rugir autour du réprouvé encore vivant.[18]

His plea almost succeeds in wrenching the other out of the abyss in which his pride has trapped him, closing in on him now in an ever-tightening circle, but already a new wave of self-hatred has swept over Cénabre. Unable to resist it by facing up openly to his defeat and taking pity on his own

[17] *Ibid.*, p. 53.   [18] *Ibid.*, p. 55.

suffering, Cénabre abandons himself to it with the "fearful happiness" of a drowning man who has ceased to struggle.

> Dans l'effusion de son affreux bonheur, cette plainte, ce dernier appel n'avait pas de sens, ou du moins pour le saisir, il devait remonter peu à peu des profondeurs de sa joie. La lenteur du retour lui fit mesurer l'énormité de sa chute.[19]

Still, something in him has stirred at the sound of Chevance's appeal. It is an ever so fleeting but bitter grief that "he would never, never again experience this supernatural pity, for he would desire it no longer."[20]

After the Abbé Chevance has finally left, defeated by Cénabre's "icy words . . . harsh glance, . . . crushing force,"[21] the battle between the satanic sea and the water of life appears to be over. But it has only just begun. In the extraordinary thirty pages which follow and which conclude the first chapter, we find the novel's imposing hero settling down at his desk, as if the events of the preceding hour had been but a dream, ready to resume his work where he left off. However, what awaits him is the discovery that the chink which grace has struck in his armor of self-deception no pretense of calm and strength is able to close again. Ironically, the work in which we see him immersing himself in order to recover his self-possession is his study on Saint Thérèse of Lisieux, "the bloodiest and best defended rose in the gardens of paradise."[22] In a matter of minutes, this new "witness," summoned to confirm the imposter's pose of calm and objectivity, reveals her true function. It is to take over where the Abbé Chevance left off and by her overwhelmingly real presence to deepen the wedge that love has set out to drive between the "double"

[19] *Ibid.*, p. 56.   [20] *Ibid.*, p. 67.   [21] *Ibid.*, pp. 58, 59.
[22] *Ibid.*, p. 69.

which the Abbé Cénabre has erected to "live" in his place
and his authentic self which this double has nearly choked
to death.

By a masterly stroke, the saint whose measure the
erudite priest thinks he is taking with the formidable tools
of his learning knocks him off balance: he hears a horrible
snicker rising from his throat, unlike any sound he has ever
produced before. It is so vulgar, so bestial and uncontrollable, that he cannot recognize it as his own laughter.
It clearly belongs to "another." Humiliated to the founda-
tions of his being, he is forced to recognize in this convulsive,
involuntary outpouring of the hideous sound "a definite
and copious reality, a concrete life to which he had always
wished to remain a stranger."[23] At first, he braces himself
against it with all the power of his will and tries to suppress
it. But this time, the manifestation is so blatant, so concrete, that he can no longer evade it. He senses himself in
the grip of an alien force against which he cannot contend.

With no chance left to him now to blind himself, as he
has done so persistently in the past, to the ever-growing
chasm between his delusion and reality, Cénabre's response
is a renewed and this time almost fatal collapse.

> Encore incapable de mesurer la violence qui l'avait soulevé
> si haut pour le laisser retomber comme une pierre, il avait
> obscurément conscience d'une déperdition inouïe de ses
> forces, d'une dissipation de sa vie. Sitôt sur la pente, la
> volonté s'abandonna, l'être fléchit tout d'une pièce.[24]

As he lets the "bitter delight" of this satanic "deliverance"
engulf him, the long-suppressed spring of satanic hatred
bursts into the open at last like an abscess.

As in *Un Mauvais Rêve* and *Un Crime*, this is the moment
of explosion in which both Satan and God risk all: either
the soul for which they wage battle will be engulfed by the

[23] *Ibid.*, p. 75.   [24] *Ibid.*, p. 86.

rising sea of death or, at last recognizing it, it will recoil from it in horror and open itself to the saving tears of divine pity.

> Quelque chose, dont l'enfer est ordinairement jaloux, se donnait ici sans réserves, avec une brutalité, une insolence inouïes. Etait-ce là le cynisme d'une âme déjà perdue? N'était-ce point plutôt, par une dernière et miséricordieuse tentative, l'écluse levée aux secrets hideux de l'âme, aux pensées venimeuses étouffées vingt ans, trente ans, l'aveu forcé, involontaire, matériel, pourtant encore libérateur, la miraculeuse déviation vers l'extérieur par le geste et la voix d'une hypocrisie parvenue au dernier degré de concentration, au dernier degré de la malfaisance, désormais incompatible avec la vie, comme le ventre se délivre parfois lui-même d'un poison dont il est, d'un seul coup, saturé?[25]

The suspense Bernanos creates at this moment of crisis is a measure of the superhuman stature with which he has endowed his hero. Even under the impact of the satanic explosion, which would settle the fate, one way or the other, of any of the writer's less heroically conceived figures, Cénabre's response is merely a tightened resistance to both contestants that precludes a final victory for either one. In the course of the suicidal hour in which, after the trigger of his revolver has jammed once, he braces himself to pull it for a second time, we see grace waging battle to counter-act the satanic water's assault on him. Prying open the rigid defenses of his pride, grace induces in him a sudden flow of tears of grief over his futile life. These tears save his life by making him pause long enough for his courage to wane; but they are shut off too soon and do not succeed in dissolving the stony self-contempt to which he clings as to "the only fixed point in the all-encompassing shipwreck."[26]

[25] *Ibid.*, p. 84.   [26] *Ibid.*, p. 95.

Les larmes vinrent aux yeux de l'abbé Cénabre, ainsi qu'une eau qui perce à travers la pierre, et il en sentait l'humidité sur son visage avec une extraordinaire angoisse. . . . C'étaient comme des larmes versées en vain. La simple acceptation, l'abandon de la lutte inutile, le geste qui avoue la défaite, s'offre au vainqueur, cela seul eût ouvert la vraie source des pleurs, et il redoutait plus cette délivrance qu'aucun supplice.[27]

He emerges at the end of the night, still held together, if only outwardly, by the sheer strength of the hatred he bears himself for his weakness, and resolved to put an end to his anxiety and to the tricks it has been playing him by going away. The chapter ends on the morning of his flight. Once more, however, as he sits on the café terrace in the early hours of the morning—those "divine" hours in the Bernanosian diurnal cycle—the same tears overcome him:

. . . à mesure que ruisselait entre ses doigts . . . cette eau solennelle, toute fatigue coulait avec elle, et il sentait frémir en lui une force immense, contre laquelle sa volonté déchue se roidissait à grand'peine.[28]

The second part of *L'Imposture* offers a glimpse of the world in which the Abbé Cénabre has been and will be seeking refuge from the water of heaven that is pursuing him. It is one of those chapters in which Bloy's influence on the early works of Bernanos is still discernible and which one wishes Bernanos had not written, or else had rewritten at a later time. Bernanos' rage was like a hurricane and, wherever it found its way into his writing untamed by his marvelous compassion and mature artistic judgment, its effect is merely painful. The bishop of Paumes, the sinister Catani, and Guérou (who is a blend of Ganse and Proust's Baron de Charlus) are caricatures. Nevertheless, the scene in which we see Pernichon destroyed by their venom and

[27] *Ibid.*, p. 95.   [28] *Ibid.*, p. 102.

ennui, provides an important background for Cénabre's tragedy. Placed into strong relief by them, he emerges as a figure of heroic proportions whose tragic defiance of the water is explained at least in part by the revolting sight of their inner "liquidation."

In the third part, the satanic element retains the upper hand. Cénabre has returned to Paris after a six months' stay in Germany in that state of "absolute calm and definitive immobility which follows a storm."[29] He firmly believes that he has so radically divested himself of the last lingering traces of self-deception, so fully faced up to the fraudulence of his vocation, that life can hold no more surprises for him. He is sure, on the strength of his now lucid rejection of faith, of being secure forever in the stronghold of his own pride and will and of being able to safeguard the secret of his apostasy until the end.

> La blessure s'était refermée, dès qu'il avait osé se regarder en face, se définir une fois pour toutes. Il ne croyait plus. Il avait totalement perdu la foi.[30]

But his self-delusion has merely reached a deeper level. If he is no longer blind to the mask he is wearing, he is now suffering from an even more dangerous form of spiritual blindness—the assumption that it is possible for a human being to live and breathe calmly under this mask and to make his peace with death. The more vigilantly he strives to maintain the outer perfection of his vocation and to seal off his inner life from all intrusions, the more relentlessly we see the inner soil of his spirit being washed away by the satanic water. His calm gives way to a raging thirst for destruction.

The movement of this chapter is an ever-accelerated "return." The at first occasional inner turmoil which

[29] *Ibid.*, p. 191.   [30] *Ibid.*, p. 194.

Cénabre cannot explain to himself and attempts to attribute to a last remnant of the crisis he thinks he has long ago overcome—lapses of memory, fits of terror, especially at the moment of consecration during mass, sudden signs of negligence in the performance of his duties—begins to take over his life. It is the composite of all his repressed, never truly outgrown phobias and childhood terrors, which now re-emerge to the surface with an infinitely potentiated, tyrannical force.

> Ces désordres . . . étaient sa vie même, poursuivant son cours implacable, cherchant sa voie et son issue, ainsi qu'une eau sous la terre.[31]

They break down the "laborious creation" of his double which his overstrained will no longer has the strength to sustain and sweep him back to a far-distant past:

> Il reculait vers le passé . . . il remontait vers sa source. Il ne découvrait pas un homme nouveau, il retrouvait l'ancien, il se retrouvait peu à peu. . . . La forte image qu'il avait formée, le personnage d'artifice et de fraude que tous—et lui-même—tenaient pour l'homme véritable et vivant, se désagrégeait petit à petit, se détachait de lui par lambeaux. Il semblait que cette laborieuse création de son industrie, amenée à son point de perfection, s'effondrât. . . .[32]

There is neither vacuum nor arrest in the dynamic Bernanosian universe. At the point where pride—which is but "the name given to the soul that devours itself"[33]—has eroded Cénabre's inner life completely, the deserted and desecrated vessel of grace cannot remain empty. The satanic flood invades and absorbs it, until it is reduced to a shallow but infinitely active reflection of satanic thirst.

The episode that shatters the renegade priest's delusion that nothing is changed, that he is still able to maintain his

[31] *Ibid.*, p. 207.   [32] *Ibid.*, p. 221.   [33] *Ibid.*, p. 199.

life at an even keel, is called forth directly by his "thirst," which has become unbearable.

> Il attendait quelque chose, il ne savait quoi, quelque chose qui allait peut-être naître de son orgueil exalté jusqu'au paroxysme, crispé ainsi qu'un muscle à la limite de son effort.[34]

What he craves, and obtains, during the night which turns out to be a satanically potentiated repetition of the night depicted in Part One, is nothing less than to see and touch, in another, the slimy, hideous bottom of his own soul which has so far still eluded his full consciousness. The exploit, despite the slightly baroque manner of the narrative, is an especially poignant recurrence of the Bernanosian rape motif, in which "rich eats poor."[35] Buying the beggar's conscience with a hundred francs, Cénabre slowly draws out of the poor wretch a "flood of filth," which relieves him as if it came out of his own being.

> Il souhaitait qu'il coulât encore, qu'il achevât d'entraîner avec lui d'autres aveux, d'autres mensonges, impossibles à atteindre jusqu'alors au fond ténébreux de sa propre conscience. . . .[36]

In the depths of the beggar's degradation, Cénabre finally glimpses, as in a mirror, the intoxicating, poisonous spring, for the thirst for which everything else has become pallid and insipid to him. It reveals to him the profoundness of his own fall, the abysmal and long-suppressed knowledge of the evil which has gained possession of him. In an orgy of "drinking," like a man who has curbed his thirst too long, Cénabre cannot let go of his prey but violates his victim even to the beggar's last saving grace: the unconsciousness that has kept the poor liar from being overwhelmed by the degree of his debasement:

[34] *Ibid.*, p. 201.   [35] *Ibid.*, p. 241.   [36] *Ibid.*, p. 226.

Visiblement, pour la première fois sans doute, cet animal humain dégradé, ainsi qu'une épave monte à la surface avant de s'engloutir à jamais, s'interrogeait sans se comprendre.[37]

When the beggar finally collapses in an epileptic fit, Cénabre has the triumph of seeing

. . . ainsi que dans un remous de l'eau profonde, l'âme traquée, forcée enfin.[38]

At the end of part three, we find Cénabre staggering back to his house like a drunkard. But before he falls asleep, he has a hallucination of thirst. The unquenchable thirst of the satanic abyss is all that is left him of the

. . . joie amère, détestable, connue de lui seul, incommunicable, d'avoir touché le fond de sa propre conscience, d'avoir prodigieusement abusé de son âme. . . .[39]

The poignant fourth and final part of *L'Imposture* depicts the divine response to the satanic triumph in the third. It too pictures a hallucination. The Abbé Chevance is dying, alone in his miserable room, and has nearly lost consciousness. Throughout his last bitter trial, which, like most of the death agonies of Bernanos' saints, is a combination of almost unbearable physical suffering, human solitude, and the anguish of having been abandoned and discarded by God as unworthy, the old priest remains true to himself. He who has never throughout his poor and laborious life worried about himself, watched himself, spent his time in self-reflection, withstands the bitterness of his final hours through "a miracle of gentleness, self-abandonment, and docility." With the innocence of a child

. . . il s'était livré du premier coup, incapable d'imaginer nulle défense, non pas seulement résigné à souffrir, mais dans l'extraordinaire ingénuité de son coeur, à souffrir petitement, bassement, lâchement, et à scandaliser le prochain.[40]

[37] *Ibid.*,p. 242.　　[38] *Ibid.*, p. 243.　　[39] *Ibid.*, p. 246.　　[40] *Ibid.*, p. 265.

As the deep springs of the Abbé Chevance's life are seen ebbing away, until nothing is left him and he dies empty, in a state of total divestment, the fundamental difference becomes apparent that sets apart the "cursed path" of Bernanos' great rebels from the equally or even more painful path of his vessels of grace. Whereas the rebel's characteristic movement, when confronted by the sea, is a turning back on the self in order that he may defend and consolidate his strength and ward off any encroachment on his proud autonomy, the saint responds to the unfathomable undercurrents of his life with a marvelous suppleness and *disponibilité*. Both must suffer pain; but whereas the first condemns himself to slow asphyxiation and the barren tortures of satanic thirst, the second, when awakened in the course of his journey to a piercing awareness of the opaqueness and distance that separate his imperfect, earthly being from the Father who is the source of his life, does not let the abyss divert his glance. He faces up to the terrible risks of his journey and accepts his absolute dependence on the water of grace by which the Father has promised to sustain him. He knows that only by resisting the spell of satanic delusion that abolishes the agonizing sense of distance and of the self's finiteness and by consenting to suffer the thirst and pain of earth will he release the deep springs of life in his soul and be able to cross the sea of death unharmed.

> Comprenez-moi, monsieur le chanoine [Chevance has tried to explain to Cénabre in the first part], nous sommes si malheureux . . . qu'il arrive que notre vie tout entière soit—à notre insu—comme . . . dérivée, en quelque sorte de Dieu au diable. Je m'exprime mal: imaginons plutôt une source perdue dans une terre aride et souillée. Ce que le Seigneur nous octroie, je dis de plus précieux: les souffrances du corps et de l'esprit, l'usage que nous en faisons, à la longue, peut les avoir corrompues. Oui! l'homme a souillé jusqu'à la substance même du coeur divin: la douleur. Le sang qui coule de la Croix peut nous tuer.[41]

41 *Ibid.*, p. 62.

Chevance's death agony is conceived as a re-enactment of and participation in the mystery of Christ's Passion, in which the infinite separation between Father and Son, the all-powerful and the most vulnerable and abandoned, is overcome by the pure and gloriously lavish outflowing of Christ's own lifeblood. Devoid of any consolation that might help to sustain him in his terrible final encounter with death and "having never known any other remedy to his troubles than to pour out to others, even in the depth of sadness, the amazing consolations of a heart consumed by paternal love,"[42] the dying old priest is haunted by a vision of the far-away Paradise into which he must lead his hungry children who are crying for milk. He too is thirsty, but unlike the satanic thirst that destroys, his is the thirst of love that is quenched only by his spending, to the last drop, his own "mystical blood."[43]

C'est le paradis. J'y conduirai mes enfants, mes pauvres enfants. . . . Il faudrait beaucoup de lait . . . beaucoup de lait. . . . Il y a du lait qui se perd. . . . Il coule à côté du seau, dans l'herbe, une mousse blanche, la rosée l'efface peu à peu. Tant de lait gâché! . . . Qu'est-ce que vous voulez que je dise à des gens qui meurent de faim?[44]

He is momentarily released from his anguish by the fierceness of his physical pain. Its irresistible, immediate power purges him of all preoccupation with past or distant things and restores him to the one thing that matters: the present moment. Suddenly, this present moment, which is all that is left him, assumes the shape of a person: it is the Abbé Cénabre whose secret has been entrusted to him and who needs him desperately.

Il restait le présent, mais libre, intact, aussi frais et neuf que s'il n'eût jamais reposé jadis dans le trouble et douteux avenir—et ce présent, c'était en somme le seul Cénabre, vers lequel ses vieilles jambes le portaient si vite. . . .[45]

[42] *Ibid.*, p. 267.   [43] *Ibid.*, p. 268.   [44] *Ibid.*, p. 280.
[45] *Ibid.*, p. 301.

In the last part of his prophetic hallucination, after a frightful and interminable taxi ride through the labyrinthine streets of Paris, the old man finally reaches Cénabre, only to see himself defeated again. He is once again rebuffed by Cénabre's icy glance of hatred, which reverses their roles and puts off on Chevance the curse of taking the serpent's part and robbing Cénabre of his peace. The possessed priest cannot forgive Chevance for having robbed him of his secret, for having found the one, fatal chink in his armor that has been keeping him alive and in torment:

> Si vous n'étiez pas au monde, petite vipère, je serais désormais hors de jeu.[46]

At last the old priest has drained his cup of sorrow. In a beautiful transition, we see him awakening from the terrible vision of his futile struggle to find himself enveloped in a blue haze,

> . . . pareille à une eau impalpable, aérienne, dont le regard atténué du moribond recueillit toute la fraîcheur. . . .[47]

Its source is Chantal de Clergerie's presence by his bedside. The young girl has been watching over him and witnessing with a kind of terror the brutal stripping of all hope and comfort which her spiritual father and friend has been suffering at the hands of death. A final, ineffable exchange takes place between the girl, who until this point has remained untouched by even a shadow of doubt or grief, and the old man whose loving wisdom has been her sole support and whose inner spring is now so spent that it cannot sustain him in his final trial. Through the gift of her fresh, undaunted joy, he dies a peaceful death; and in turn she receives in trust, without knowing it, the heavy burden which he has struggled, seemingly in vain, to redeem: the secret of the Abbé Cénabre's apostasy.

[46] *Ibid.*, p. 307.   [47] *Ibid.*, p. 308.

The fifth and last part of Cénabre's drama unfolds in *La Joie*. Though he is absent from the first half of the novel and does not re-emerge to the foreground till the second part, Cénabre is nevertheless the figure around whom fundamentally revolves and on whom converges the mysterious story of the passion of Chantal de Clergerie. *La Joie* should have been Bernanos' greatest work. Its scope is extraordinary, encompassing as it does the journey of a spiritually gifted girl from her first joyful glimpse of Paradise; through a world of men who "prefer cold to hot" and whose perverse "thirst" for self-destruction the infinite spring of God's own love cannot redeem and quench save by spending itself to the last, to death; to her agony in the Garden of Olives, in which, in a final outflowing of the deepest springs of her life, she redeems Cénabre from the satanic abyss. As it stands, it is an uneven work, parts of which may justify Bernanos' own disappointed remark that it is a Magnificat that does not sing. But its best pages match the level of his masterpiece *Journal d'un curé de campagne* both in evocative power and depth of vision.

From the opening of the first part of *La Joie*, Cénabre's hidden presence is evoked in and around the Norman country house that provides the setting of Chantal's story. Everything surrounding the young girl suggests massive deception, impenetrable "evil dreams," and weight. Her father is a little man devoured by ambition, a hoarder of fame who anxiously wards off any claims that anyone, including his daughter, might make on his concern, lest he find himself distracted from his perennial, piercing worry about himself. The insane grandmother is a pure embodiment of satanic thirst. Chained to the past by an incessant stream of ruminations in which the demons of unfulfilled greed and fear have poisoned every memory, she is a haunted creature who cannot get out from under the weight of her "inner dream" that has exiled her from the present and the living. Finally, there are the domestics, and in particular, the Russian chauffeur Fiodor, in whose cold, "thirsty" eyes Chantal reads

> . . . cette même curiosité qu'on voit au regard des bêtes savantes ou corrompues . . . lorsqu'elles flairent de loin, sur les routes, leurs congénères libres et heureux.[48]

Amidst all these, the young girl's presence calls up the image of a delicate, transparent morning foredoomed by the poisonous emanations of decay that are waiting to destroy it:

> La joie du jour, du jour en fleur, un matin d'août . . . et déjà dans l'air trop lourd, les perfides aromates d'automne. ... C'était la joie du jour, et par on ne sait quelle splendeur périssable, c'était aussi la joie d'un seul jour, le jour unique, si délicat, si fragile dans son impalpable sérénité, où paraît pour la première fois, à la cime ardente de la canicule, la brume insidieuse traînant encore au-dessus de l'horizon et qui descendra quelques semaines plus tard sur la terre épuisée, les prés défraîchis, l'eau dormante, avec l'odeur des feuillages taris.[49]

Chantal's secret is the same as that of the dead Abbé Chevance: a "radiant spirit of acceptance and abandon."[50] Incapable under any circumstances whatever of flinching from anything that she encounters on her path and entrenching herself in security within a self-created fortress, she derives her overflowing joy both from her deep faith in the Father's love and her equally deep certainty of her own smallness and powerlessness in the face of life's mighty currents. Hers is the supernatural poverty of God's chosen vessels, whose total freedom from self-reflection enables them to affront dangers which must shatter weightier and less pure beings. She is propelled not by her own limited power but by the infinite source of divine love that flows

---

[48] *La Joie*, p. 58.   [49] *Ibid.*, p. 33.   [50] *Ibid.*, p. 36.

through her and sustains her as the need arises. In contrast
to those who surround her, whose response to life is one of
hoarding and withholding, of shielding and tightening until
they are, in Fiodor's own words, "outside of life," choked
to death by their own defenses, Chantal is a divine spend-
thrift:

> . . . parmi ces visages hostiles ou clos, elle donnait, elle
> prodiguait, elle jetait à pleines mains, ainsi qu'une chose
> de rien, son espérance sublime.[51]

But soon after the death of the Abbé Chevance, who had
watched over her and allowed her to pour out her precious
gift, unaware yet of the "supernatural burden" it would
one day draw down on her, her time of untroubled innocence comes to an end. Ushered in by her first deep grief
and bewilderment at seeing the venerable old man who had
lived for love alone die as if under a curse, unrelieved by a
single drop of consolation, a terrible realization about her
own fate begins to grow in Chantal: she sees that her joy
not merely fails to give happiness to others but that they
respond to it as to an evil force, with a blind rage to capture
and destroy it. In her transcendent radiance, each one
seems to recognize with despair his own long-submerged
dream of Paradise and to measure the distance by which
the *mensonge* of his life has removed him from even desiring
its realization:

> Hélas, Madame Fernande [the Russian says to the cook],
> le secret de cette maison n'est pas le mal—non—mais la
> grâce. Nos âmes maudites la boivent comme l'eau, ne lui
> trouvent aucun goût, aucune saveur, bien qu'elle soit le feu
> qui nous consumera tous éternellement. . . . Que dire?
> Chacun de nous s'agite en vain, se débat; nous sommes pris
> entre les mailles d'un filet qui nous emporte pêle-mêle où
> nous ne voulons pas aller.[52]

[51] *Ibid.*, p. 60.   [52] *Ibid.*, p. 154.

A snare of complicity tightens around Chantal. Wherever she turns, she is aware of eyes fastened on her with the cruel desire to draw out of her the source of her joy and to poison it by projecting into it the evil currents of envy and doubt. The girl is stunned by these multiple assaults of satanic thirst. Those around her close in on her as a polluted soil encroaches on a delicate spring. We see them bent on arresting and absorbing her, not to be vivified but as if to prove at any cost the futility of her vibrant presence in their barren and deceitful world.

But Chantal refuses to turn back on herself in fear. Instead of retreating and shielding herself in revolt from this world which bears no resemblance to her Father's but appears to have been taken over by strangers and slaves, she keeps her limpid glance focused on its hidden miseries. As her own pain grows deeper, so do the immense inner resources of her love and insight.

> Voilà qu'elle s'avançait maintenant à travers un pays inconnu, hors des frontières de son ancien paradis, seule, . . . prête à faire face, et son regard aussi ferme et aussi sûr, dans son implacable pureté, que celui d'un homme intrépide. . . . Comme un homme endormi à l'aube, qui s'éveille dans la brutale lumière de midi avec encore dans ses yeux la sérénité de l'aurore, le monde qui n'était jusqu'à ce moment pour elle qu'un mot mystérieux, se révélait, non à son expérience, mais à sa charité—par l'intuition, l'épanouissement, le rayonnement de la pitié.[53]

In the course of her journey, every new confrontation with evil, while exhausting her psychologically and physically, opens to her more deeply the limitless, fiery gulf of divine compassion, draws her closer to the Father from whose eyes no human soil is impenetrable enough to conceal the suffering which love has come to redeem.

[53] *Ibid.*, pp. 47–48.

. . . déjà la plaie mystérieuse était ouverte d'où ruisselait
une charité plus humaine, plus charnelle, qui découvre
Dieu dans l'homme, et les confond l'un et l'autre, par la
même compassion surnaturelle.[54]

Her life begins to bear a mysterious resemblance to Christ's.
Steadfastly keeping her inner vision focused on the wound
she sees festering in those who bear down on her with
hatred, she is engulfed in a state of awe and grief that yet
remains pure of any bitterness. Gradually this grief, and
the cumulative strain of withstanding, without shrinking
back, the cruel tests to which she is being put, become so
overwhelming that she can no longer feel or taste the joy
that continues to emanate from her. Its source—her "divine
hope"—has come to elude her, having receded into so
deeply hidden a recess of her soul that only the Father
himself can see it and be comforted by it in those hours of
mystic contemplation when she loses all consciousness of
herself. What is left for her self-awareness is the agonizing
reflection she reads in the satanic glance of those who
question her: her inability to understand herself, her humiliating illness—her ecstasies may be of pathological origin
since there has been insanity in her family—and what is
probably a self-delusion in trusting herself to be carried to
her destination by the Father's love. As her glance exerts
its redemptive power by drawing to herself the others'
satanic glance of self-hatred and delusion and returning it
purged by love, she must in exchange expiate the curse of
their evil dreams by suffering it in its pure form as privation
of life. This poignant drama of exchange, in which a fragile
vessel of grace becomes the pivot on which the spiritual fate
of all other characters of *La Joie* is suspended, in which the
one spring of living water is sacrificed to break open and
revive the novel's petrified and rotten landscape, confirms

[54] *Ibid.*, p. 49.

Bernanos' heroic vision of humanity's own part in the divine economy of salvation. Not only does Christ answer for man in the mysterious exchange wrought in his Passion, but in the indivisible drama of mankind's own painful journey towards Paradise a supernatural justice is at work under which the spiritually rich must answer for the poor, the living spend their life blood to redeem the dead.

The ultimate test of Chantal's love, which leads to the novel's climax at the end of the second part, is prefigured in a prophetic vision. Exhausted to death, fearing that she has nothing left to give to anyone, and yet certain that the greatest crisis of her life is just ahead of her, the young girl has gone up to her room for a short respite and sunk into prayer at the foot of the crucifix. As many times before, she is transported into the Garden of Olives and there sees her own sorrow flowing into the sublime stream of Christ's redemptive blood and tears:

> Bien des fois, en effet, depuis l'enfance, elle s'était sentie portée par la pensée auprès du Dieu solitaire, réfugié dans la nuit comme un père humilié entre les bras de sa dernière fille, consommant lentement son angoisse humaine dans l'effusion du sang et des larmes, sous les noirs oliviers. . . . Alors elle se couche à ses pieds, elle s'écrase contre le sol, elle sent sur sa poitrine et ses joues l'âcre fraîcheur de la terre, cette terre qui vient de boire, avec une avidité furieuse, l'eau de ses yeux ineffables dont un seul regard, en créant l'univers, a contenu toutes les aurores et tous les soirs.[55]

But this time, no consolation is in store for her. The vision continues to expand, and suddenly she sees before her not Christ in his ineffable, life-giving love but the figure of Judas who has betrayed him and in despair has hanged himself—

[55] *Ibid.*, pp. 249–50.

... dressé à jamais, fruit noir d'un arbre noir, à l'entrée du honteux royaume de l'ombre, sentinelle exacte, incorruptible, que la miséricorde assiège en vain, qui ne laissera passer aucun pardon, pour que l'enfer consomme en paix sa paix horrible. L'arbre monte lentement au-dessus de l'horizon. . . . Elle ne voit plus qu'un tronc, une énorme colonne recouverte d'écorce, comme si l'arbre venait de se refermer sur son fruit. Toutes les larmes qu'elle écoute maintenant tomber sur la pierre ne rendraient pas une goutte de sève à ce gibet colossal.[56]

She is frozen with horror. But then she hears the gentle lament of the Christ who had to see his love rebound against the betrayer's impenetrable despair, his radiant youth sold and held captive by the other's hatred, and she sees him offering his life for the betrayer above all others. She understands that as long as she has a drop of life left to give, she must give it or else receive nothing more herself, ever. By a superhuman effort she masters her fear, advances towards the petrified giant, and offers it her life. Immediately it starts to shrink back to natural proportions and assumes the shape of a black, gnarled olive tree. She hears it crack and tremble from roots to top. Suddenly its monstrous crown breaks through the thick cover of moss and bark and, in a hideous move, closes in on her. At that moment, Chantal regains consciousness and finds the Abbé Cénabre standing before her.

The events that take place between that moment and the end of the novel are an exact enactment of Chantal's vision. A few months have elapsed between the end of *L'Imposture* and Cénabre's arrival at the Clergeries' for a holiday, at Clergerie's pressing invitation. Once again, his phenomenal will power has enabled the renegade priest to reconsolidate his defenses and to resume, with apparent calm, his fraudulent life. But in order to do so, he has had to impose

[56] *Ibid.*, pp. 253–54.

a virtual exile on himself, for all human intercourse has become hateful to him. He has retreated into the country and, giving up all pastoral duties, has devoted his time and thoughts to detached scholarly labors. A universal dislike for him has replaced people's former respect and admiration, "so hard, compact and intolerable becomes the silence which surrounds men like him."[57] When he arrives at the Clergeries', at the opening of the novel's second part, his appearance suggests something of the tomb. He associates with no one, remains silent throughout the meals, and emerges from his room only at night, when he is seen taking solitary walks in the garden. From the time of his arrival, he has avoided Chantal with particular care, treating her, on the few occasions when he has had to speak to her, with an almost exaggerated deference. Yet it is on account of her alone that he has come. Knowing of her close relationship with the Abbé Chevance, an uncontrollable impulse has been propelling him to see her and test her, to find out whether the terrible secret of his self-violation which he once let escape him is being kept alive by her.

The dramatic confrontation between the two, which takes place right after Chantal awakens from her mystic vision and finds him bending over her, is the ultimate test for both. It is a re-enactment, on the human plane, of the confrontation between Christ and Judas, in which love and hatred, each in the ineffable solitude of its own secret, seek to overcome one another. Ironically, it is Cénabre who feels sure of himself in this contest, safely ensconced in what he believes to be the definitive peace of his total renunciation of hope; and it is Chantal who feels herself to be completely at his mercy. She is not conscious of having his secret, she "has" nothing; while he, like already many others before him, thinks he has taken hold of hers and can now proceed

[57] *Ibid.*, p. 168.

to judge and condemn her as someone who is a danger to the peace of mind of others. But before he realizes what is happening to him, her very innocence that eludes his avid questions deals his self-delusion a new blow. It lays bare once again the deep anguish or thirst of a man who secretly knows himself to be living suspended over a chasm, who is suffocating underneath the massive superstructure of his *mensonge*:

> Cette colère inattendue, cet ébranlement de tout l'être vers un obstacle en apparence si fragile, n'éveillait pas sa méfiance. Il n'y reconnaissait point la même frénésie qui l'avait précipité sur l'abbé Chevance, ou traîné une nuit entière aux talons d'un vieux mendiant, en proie à toutes les fureurs homicides.[58]

Cénabre brutally accuses Chantal of being a temptation to others, of "posing a problem for which she cannot offer a solution," and advises her, for her own good, to protect herself a little better. When, in reply, Chantal only asks sadly, "Is there no place for me then, anywhere?" he is so shaken by the purity of her grief, by the total absence of any sign of despair or revolt in her, that the agony of his own, self-imposed, exile breaks once again into the open:

> —Ni pour vous, ni pour moi. . . . Bref, pour des raisons différentes, nous sommes de ces gens qui ne peuvent subsister à découvert, doivent chercher un abri, et nul abri n'est sûr si un autre en connaît le chemin.[59]

"Are we to lie then?" she asks him. Carried away now by his anguish and bent on crushing her, he assaults her with all the awesome power of his satanic delusion of autonomy and power:

> Ce sont les derniers réduits où peuvent tenir ceux d'entre nous qui ne se donnent point à garder, qui se gardent eux-mêmes, ont trouvé par leurs propres moyens l'axe de leur vie, leur point fixe et secret. Je suis de ceux-là.[60]

[58] *Ibid.*, p. 260.   [59] *Ibid.*, p. 272.   [60] *Ibid.*, p. 273.

However, Chantal's reply cannot but make him see the sterility and crushing weight of the fate he has chosen. In all her terror at being abused and drained of her strength, she is free. She has nothing to save or protect from anyone. To her, her very emptiness is a sign that her struggle is nearing its end, that she is approaching her destination:

> Me voilà maintenant jetée dans le pressoir: Dieu tirera de moi par force ce que je n'aurais pas le courage de donner. Rien désormais ne l'arrêtera. Il me semblait tout à l'heure que sa sainte pitié s'éloignait de moi . . . et je sens bien que je ne la retrouverai plus qu'en paradis. Dès lors tout m'est égal, voyez-vous, absolument. . . . Plus j'approche du but, moins je souhaite le connaître.[61]

In a mysterious exchange, we see Chantal relieving the renegade priest of the burden of his apostasy and letting it bear down on her in all its horror. What she sees of his life is not the concealing mask or bark but the parched living being underneath who is now breaking through, tortured by thirst. Her supernatural pity, flowing out to him as he tempts her, challenges her, defies her, is like a stream of pure water which he cannot resist and which he drains to the last drop. So immense is its purifying power that as it meets the *mensonge* or evil dream of his life a faint glimmer of hope, part of the authentic dream of Paradise, begins to shine through. When the girl asks his forgiveness for having perhaps provoked his confession against his will, his answer strikes an utterly new note. "A moment ago, it was still just an ordinary secret. What will it become in your hands?"[62] A communion has been established between her life and his, which he accepts with strange eagerness. As they leave her room together, he remarks quietly, seeing her anguished face, "We are leaving the night behind, yet the day is not less difficult to overcome."[63]

---

[61] *Ibid.*, p. 277.   [62] *Ibid.*, p. 283.   [63] *Ibid.*, p. 284.

Cénabre's final attempt to flee, to escape at all costs from the mercy that is now pouring into him from all sides, proves futile. As he leans out of the window in the oppressive summer night, a raindrop falls on his hand,

> . . . chaude, pesante, parfumée comme une goutte de nard, et qui était l'essence même du jour évanoui.[64]

The "fading day" is Chantal's life. As the explosion of evil, her murder by the Russian chauffeur, becomes imminent—in a development that seems, alas, somewhat contrived—all those who should be protecting her, in particular her father and the psychiatrist who knows about the Russian's criminal tendencies, run away on one pretext or another and abandon her to her fate. Cénabre himself has a clear premonition of the murder, and in a last satanic impulse of defiance longs for it in order that he may regain full possession of himself. But his longing is deceived: the shock of the brutal murder that takes place minutes after the girl's father has left by train precipitates the final collapse of his will and reason. No sooner has the crime taken place, than Cénabre, in a "sudden explosion of terror," feels himself pierced to the heart.

> Le coup avait été porté du dehors. . . . Oui, hors de lui, hors de son pouvoir, un événement venait de naître—qu'il ne connaissait point, qu'il ne connaîtrait peut-être jamais. . . . Lequel? . . . Il semblait que tout contrôle lui fût retiré de sa propre conscience, qu'il ne fût désormais plus le maître d'aucun de ces secrets que le plus grossier des hommes sait encore défendre contre la curiosité d'autrui.[65]

With shattering certainty he knows himself henceforth "broken open, unable to retain a single falsehood," and under the unbearable strain of this humiliation his mind gives way. All he experiences is "a flood of light" which he

[64] *Ibid.*, p. 300.   [65] *Ibid.*, p. 303.

cannot ward off. When the cook Fernande calls to him for help and they discover in Chantal's brightly lit room the bodies of the young girl and her murderer, Cénabre's anguish wipes out the last vestige of his fraudulent double and releases a pure, "sovereign grief." His last words, spoken in the darkness of complete human shipwreck, are the opening words of the Lord's Prayer.

{ Il était debout, face aux ténèbres, seul, et comme à la proue
d'un navire.
                    Sous le Soleil de Satan

V.

The Garden of Olives

The first-born and most intrepid of Bernanos' vessels of
grace, whom we see exhausting himself in the struggle to
overcome the deep currents of the sea and to steer the
human race closer to the Father's kingdom—glimpsed in
all its splendor in the early, transparent joy of childhood—
is, paradoxically, as parched and thirst-wracked a figure as
any of the novelist's great rebels. In creating Donissan, the
towering rebel-saint of Lumbres, in a first burst of creative
passion, Bernanos accomplished the feat of fashioning one
of his most abundant fountains of grace out of the same
rock which was going to go, two years later, into the making
of Cénabre. To appreciate the organic oneness of the
Bernanosian human landscape, in which not only the
hidden springs of divine love and satanic hatred but also
the seemingly most irreconcilable earthly figures, from the
most massively defiant to the most gentle and transparent,
are bound up with one another in an all-encompassing
drama, one need only take a close look at Donissan. He is
of a different cast than his remarkable progeny—Chantal
de Clergerie, the Abbé Chevance,[1] or the curé d'Ambricourt, who for all their strength emerge as tender, fluid

[1] Cf. chapter 4.

figures, distinguished by a heavenly docility in the hands of their divine creator. In contrast to them, Donissan still shares with the great rebels, in particular with Cénabre and the Mouchette of the Prologue to his own story, for whose sake he is led into his awful "detour" into the satanic abyss, a massive defiance and willfulness that very nearly propel him into the gaping jaw of the Enemy.

Everything about the sorrowful figure of the young peasant priest bears the sign of wrath and of a will strained to its limits. "Everything is a trap and a scandal to him."[2] From his earliest childhood, he tells his spiritual father, the Abbé Menou-Segrais, he has "lived less in hope of the glory which we will possess one day, than in sorrow over the glory which we have lost."[3] From his first glimpse of the fearful distance which separates the desert in which he finds himself from the promised land of fountains, he is in the grip of terror. He is unable to trust and abandon himself to the mysterious grace that has been given him and that streams out of him through his heavy and clumsy outer shell, and so he stiffens himself defiantly. All he can see is his ineptness, the hateful inadequacy of his natural resources to measure up to his vocation, and underlying it, the irresistible current of satanic hatred which keeps sweeping him off his true course and threatens to turn the distance into an unbridgeable chasm.

> A certaines heures, voir est à soi seul une épreuve si dure, qu'on voudrait que Dieu brisât le miroir. On le briserait, mon ami. . . .[4]

In the relentless battle he wages against the hostile thirsty water, we see Donissan's glance, which time and again frees others from the blinding reflections of the abyss,

---

[2] *Sous le Soleil de Satan*, p. 139.
[3] *Ibid.*, p. 238.
[4] *Ibid.*, p. 283.

turn against him and threaten to arrest and reverse his own course. The blindness that his transparent purity of soul lifts from others strikes him in their place. All he can see of himself, as he strains and labors with a crushing sense of his unworthiness that is dangerously close to self-hatred, is the face of his double, the evil reflection of himself which the Serpent holds out to him to destroy him. In this satanically reversed image, the deep, overflowing joy that is God's greatest gift to him and his one and only source of sustenance is seen by him as a perfidious temptation to give up the struggle and to surrender to Satan's snare. In the satanic mirror, he sees his divine hope as presumption and his solitude in his mighty struggle as a "land of exile" to which God has condemned his unfaithful servant:

> Il a fui sans le savoir la divine main tendue—la vision même du visage plein de reproche—puis le dernier cri au-dessus des collines, le suprême appel lointain, aussi faible qu'un soupir. Chaque pas l'enfonce plus avant dans la terre d'exile.[5]

All of Bernanos' protagonists share in some measure the sense of damnation that, in striking contrast to the antagonists' delusion of peace and freedom, is one of the surest signs of their participation in the mystery of Christ's Passion. The saint who is himself a fountain of grace must, in exchange for the precious gift of life he dispenses to others—liberation from the deep waters of self-hatred—call down upon himself the curse of Satan's thirsty water, compared to which the desert itself is an oasis. But in this saint, Donissan, who still bears all the marks of Bernanos' early, tempestuous despair, the sense of damnation is aggravated by a natural temperament more suitable for a warrior or insurgent than for a saint. His natural impulse is to defy, to attack by force, and where he cannot hope to vanquish,

[5] *Ibid.*, p. 123.

to resist with every fiber of his being, until he is one solid
mass of resistance and thus unwittingly becomes a perfect
target for the enemy.

> Hi! Hi! Hi [the devil taunts him]! De tous ceux que j'ai vus
> marqués du même signe que toi, tu es le plus lourd, le plus
> obtus, le plus compact! . . . Tu creuses ton sillon comme un
> boeuf, tu bourres sur l'ennemi comme un bouc. . . . De haut
> en bas, une bonne cible![6]

Ironically, from the first major point of departure in
Donissan's spiritual journey, when after years of seemingly
hopeless exertions to overcome his clumsiness and "stu-
pidity" and to satisfy his superiors, the Abbé Menou-
Segrais finally enables Donissan to perceive his magnificent
gifts and releases in him the deep, mysterious joy of knowing himself loved and chosen by the Father, we see a
warrior pulled down by the weight of his own armor into
the snare of the "powers from below." So great is the
humiliated, inarticulate young peasant's suspicion of himself and, consequently, of the immense wave of love that
promises to carry him beyond himself, to shore, sweeping
all obstacles aside in its magnificent *élan*, that he does not
dare relax his own will and entrust himself to it fully.

> . . . il en jouissait avec une avidité craintive, comme d'un
> périlleux tresor que le maître inconnu va reprendre, d'une
> minute à l'autre, et qu'on ne peut déjà laisser sans mourir.[7]

Almost immediately after this departure we see him tightening up again and refusing, with the tragic defiance of the
"bad poor man at the banquet," the splendor he has been
invited to share. The gap between his poverty and this
splendor is too great; it crushes him. Only a miracle of
docility and self-forgetfulness would enable him to surrender to this joy and let it carry him on its crest, like a light,

---

[6] *Ibid.*, p. 179.   [7] *Ibid.*, p. 121.

mobile raft, into the Father's garden. But Donissan bears too deeply within him the mark of Satan's curse. He turns back in self-reflection at the very moment when his gaze should be focused on the ineffable vision before him, and, seeing himself as a tempted and despicable wretch, rejects that vision with horror as a delusion.

> L'âme aride, qui ne connut jamais d'autre douceur qu'une tristesse muette et résignée, s'étonne, puis s'effraie, enfin s'irrite contre cette inexplicable suavité. A la premiere étape de l'ascension mystique, le coeur manque au misérable pris de vertige, et de toutes ses forces il essaiera de rompre ce recueillement passif, le silence intérieur dont l'apparente oisiveté le déconcerte.... Le pauvre prêtre croit flairer le piège tendu. . . . Cette joie sans cause ne peut être qu'une illusion. . . . *Il lui faut déraciner cette joie!*[8]

Blinded by the satanic reflection, he mistakes the spring of divine love and hope for the treacherous deep water of perdition and turns against it in a paroxysm of hatred, "in which the love which has been betrayed is no longer good for anything but destruction. . . . He hated his whole being. He hated himself with the hatred of a man unable to survive his dream."[9] In the passage that depicts the brutal flagellation which the saint inflicts on himself that night under the spell of his delusion, the hissing, writhing chain with which he almost kills himself becomes a live embodiment of the Serpent whose hatred has marked him for destruction.

All through the novel, we see the sign of ambiguity casting its deep shadow over Donissan's heroic figure and literally splitting him in two. Of all of Bernanos' protagonists, he is the most threatened and strife-torn, the most cruelly divided. In actuality an inexhaustible fountain of tender, paternal love for his children whom he leads into

[8] *Ibid.*, pp. 129–30.   [9] *Ibid.*, p. 132.

the Father's Garden by his tears and sweat, he must bear the curse of regarding himself as a parched tree in the heart of a desert, which is preserved from collapse only by its tenacious power of resistance. The rhythm of Donissan's dramatic journey is marked by an alternation of violent expansions and contractions, of breathtaking advances towards the Father followed by deep plunges into the satanic abyss. For each inspired moment of his extraordinary life, when he frees a sinner from his prison of self-deception and restores him to the truth in which all suffering is redemptive because it is testimony to the Father of man's unquenchable longing for him, the saint pays with an agonizing sense of depletion and inner barrenness. The evil that in others his vision has purged and transformed into a pure outcry for the Father's love, bears down on him in turn in all its unredeemed opaqueness. It turns the world into a cursed desert in which, wherever he turns, he can detect nothing but the ubiquitous, gloating triumph of the other, the Father's double, whose bottomless ennui he must either defy to the death, or perish.

A redeemer of others, Donissan thus nearly becomes his own destroyer. Repeatedly, in subtle, almost imperceptible shifts, we see the embattled saint, weary and dizzy after an overwhelming wave of grace has flung him far out of his depth, recoil into a state of armed hostility in which he becomes a stranger to the world. This satanic metamorphosis is superbly evoked in each of the crucial episodes through a sudden shift in the direction of the hero's glance. We see it first in the Christmas night; then in the Devil's revelation to him of the special mark of his election; again at the end of that same night, in his encounter with Mouchette, which forms the novel's central event; and finally in the opening of "Le Saint de Lumbres" and his last trial, the resurrection scene. In each of these episodes, his vision of love is seen shadowed or "doubled" by its satanic counterpart, which seeks to reverse its effect.

The movement of the authentic glance of love is a giving, outflowing one in which the saint transmits to another the life-giving "azure gulf" of divine love that is his own deepest source of sustenance.

> . . . comme le rayonnement d'une lueur secrète, comme l'écoulement à travers lui d'une source inépuisable de clarté, une sensation inconnue, infiniment subtile et pure, sans aucun mélange, atteignait peu à peu jusqu'au principe de la vie, le transformait dans sa chair même. Ainsi qu'un homme mourant de soif s'ouvre tout entier à la fraîcheur aigue de l'eau, il ne savait si ce qui l'avait comme transpercé de part en part était plaisir ou douleur.[10]

It is a movement in which the giver offers himself together with the gift and is absorbed by the subject. The precise nature of this movement of the saint's vision is evoked in one superb passage of *Sous le Soleil de Satan*: Donissan has barely emerged from the first major round of his duel with the Devil when the divine gift, with the "double" of which Satan has tempted him in vain, is revealed to him in its most blissful form. As he walks behind his good Samaritan who has found him unconscious on the road and is going back with him toward Campagne in the darkness, his soul is suddenly transported within the innermost soul of his companion and he is able to see it with perfect clarity:

> Il voyait devant lui son compagnon, il le voyait à n'en douter pas, bien qu'il ne distinguât point ses traits, qu'il cherchât vainement son visage ou ses mains. . . . Et néanmoins, sans rien craindre, il regardait l'extraordinaire clarté avec une confiance sereine, une fixité calme, non point pour la pénétrer, mais sûr d'être pénétré par elle. . . . ce ne fut qu'un éclair. . . . Chacun doit *descendre* en soi-même et à mesure qu'il descend, les ténèbres s'épaississent jusqu'au tuf obscur,

[10] *Ibid.*, p. 193.

au moi profond, où s'agitent les ombres des ancêtres, où mugit l'instinct ainsi qu'une eau sous la terre. Et voilà que ce misérable prêtre se trouvait soudain transporté au plus intime d'un autre être, sans doute à ce point même où porte le regard du juge. Il avait conscience du prodige, et il était dans le ravissement que ce prodige fut si simple, et sa révélation si douce. . . . Sans pouvoir l'exprimer . . . il sentait que cette connaissance était selon sa nature, que l'intelligence et les facultés dont s'enorgueillissent les hommes y avaient peu de part, qu'elle était seulement et simplement l'effervescence, l'expansion, la dilatation de la charité. . . . L'entreprise etait si simple, au fond, et le but si proche. . . . L'aveugle quand il a pris possession du nouveau sens qui lui est rendu, ne s'étonne pas plus de toucher du regard le lointain horizon qu'il n'atteignait jadis qu'avec tant de labeur, à travers les fondrières et les ronces.[11]

But, tragically, as the outflowing vision which carries with it all his own human strength is fated to encounter time and again not innocence but the dense morass of human weakness in the grip of satanic delusion, which threatens to absorb it without profit, we see that vision retract itself sharply and succumb to its own shadow. The gentle outflow turns then into an assault, in which the saint, now abusing his gift with a vengeance, sets out to master and vanquish. His vision becomes a form of satanic thirst. A blind reflex, engendered by the need to steady himself and regain possession of himself, makes him turn against the subject before him in a rage of destruction. Before his eyes, the subject is suddenly divested of its identity and transformed into an enemy, or rather into an anonymous reflection of the Enemy that must be seized and obliterated before it can extend the Enemy's power any further.

[11] *Ibid.*, pp. 185, 186, 187.

Il est vaincu. Par la brèche ouverte, l'orgueil rentre à flots dans son coeur. . . . L'autre concupiscence s'éveille, ce délire de la connaissance. . . . Connaître pour détruire, et renouveler dans la destruction sa connaissance et son désir—ô soleil de Satan![12]

Not one of Bernanos' later protagonists suffers the same cruel oscillation between transparent love and blind hatred. It is the special curse of this one who is marked for battle, whose apparent vocation it is not merely to withstand Satan's blinding power while leading his thirsty and weary fellows to the Father but to assault Satan actively, "to pursue him in men's souls," at the risk of losing his own direction and salvation. Donissan's battle is an impossible wager no man, not even this giant, can hope to win. For as his glance recklessly seeks to take hold of and pin down the elusive Adversary in the human being before him, its power to embrace the latter's captive self and thus set it free is hopelessly jeopardized. Time and again, because of his presumption, this passionate lover not only of the Father but of his most derelict children is fated to see himself defeated both in his hatred and, worse still, in his love which he has allowed that hatred to invade. His glance, in its pursuit of the Enemy, succeeds only in piercing the subject from top to bottom and in ending up, to its dismay, in the bottomless thirsty void of the Serpent's eye:

Celui qui, noué des deux mains à la pointe extrême du mât, perdant tout à coup l'équilibre gravitationnel, verrait se creuser et s'enfler sous lui, non plus la mer, mais tout l'abîme sidéral, et bouillante à des trillions de lieues, l'écume des nébuleuses en gestation, au travers du vide que rien ne mesure et que va traverser sa chute éternelle, ne sentirait pas au creux de sa poitrine un vertige plus absolu. . . .[13]

[12] *Ibid.*, pp. 255–57.   [13] *Ibid.*, pp. 170–71.

Until the last, we see the saint's agile Adversary mocking
him, as Donissan's blasting attacks miss their target and,
after nearly destroying the very beings whom they are
designed to save, rebound on himself and pommel him into
near-surrender. Too defiant and too massive to slip through
the Devil's snares, as Chantal or the curé d'Ambricourt will
be able to do after him, the saint is blinded and either sees
himself downright defeated by his foe or else, in several
crucial rounds of their duel, is left in such cruel uncertainty
over the outcome that even a clear defeat would be a lesser
torment to him.

This curse of blindness that marks the life of the rebel-
saint of Lumbres whose quest for Paradise encompasses
some of the deepest, most treacherous falls or "returns"
into nothingness testifies more sharply and brutally than
any other Bernanosian element to the Father's own eclipse,
in the realm of human time, by the star of the fallen Angel.
Such is the blinding power of Satan in the novel in which
he emerges in person as the invincible Antagonist that even
the most solid realities of life—individual beings, specific
places, moments, events—which the saint's love seeks out,
passionately, in order to bring them to fruition and give
them their rightful place in the Father's Garden, keep dissolving before his eyes.

Through his own falls into the depths of satanic delusion,
Donissan becomes, in a special way, a brother and redeemer
of all the great Bernanosian rebels. His tortuous path
appears especially patterned to meet and redeem theirs. It
thus offers, in its very tortuousness, the most moving
testimony to love Bernanos has conceived, by showing there
is no depth, no chaos, into which love will not venture.

> Où il vous mène, on sent qu'il monte avec vous. La dure
> vérité, qui tout à coup d'un mot longtemps cherché, court
> vous atteindre en pleine poitrine, l'a blessé avant vous.[14]

[14] *Ibid.*, p. 117.

The Prologue, which on a first reading may strike the reader as somehow extraneous to the body of the novel, is in fact Bernanos' evocation of the *raison d'être* of Donissan's battle. In the story of the intrepid sixteen-year-old Mouchette, who is the forerunner of all of Bernanos' orphaned and desperate children, the triumph of the world's false father becomes an immediate and dramatic reality. It is a symbolic story. The girl's exuberant departure in quest of joy and of a hero, and her recoil in defiant despair when she finds only a seducer and the irony of a world in which one gets nowhere because it is "round as a ball," are symbolic of humanity's humiliating experience of defeat in its quest for Paradise. No sooner has the child set out to reach the Paradise she has glimpsed on a radiant spring morning in the beloved familiar landscape,

> . . . la forêt de Sauves, la colline bleue, et la grande plaine vers la mer, avec le soleil sur les dunes . . .[15]

than she is led in an infernal circle right back to where she started, the house of the despicable petty tyrant who is her father, and is left there to suffocate in silence:

> Hélas! comme un enfant, parti le matin pour découvrir un nouveau monde, fait le tour du potager, et se retrouve auprès du puits, ayant vu périr son premier rêve, ainsi n'avait-elle fait que ce petit pas inutile hors de la route commune. . . .[16]

The image that sums up her shipwrecked dream is the fundamental one, recurring persistently throughout the writer's works, of "a fragile vessel in the wind"[17] that has no sooner hoisted its sails than it capsizes and sinks to the bottom of the sea.

> La vie un moment ouverte, déployée de toute l'envergure, le vent de l'espace frappant en plein, . . . puis repliée, retombant à pic comme une pierre.[18]

[15] *Ibid.*, p. 15.   [16] *Ibid.*, p. 40.   [17] *Ibid.*, p. 218.   [18] *Ibid.*, p. 54.

The circular movement of her journey, in the course of which her whole being is slowly reduced to a senseless echo and reflection of hatred in which "another pleases and admires himself," symbolizes the almost irresistible tide that throughout Bernanos' fictional universe keeps sweeping his humanity back from its inspired pursuit of the pure spring of love into the chasm of its blind terrors. It transforms the clear spring of Mouchette's dream of Paradise into a stagnant pool crawling with millepedes:

> Je te connais [she tells Gallet, her vulgar middle-aged lover to whom she has, with a mixture of pleading and satanic defiance, confided her impulse to drown herself in the nearby pond]. Tu n'aimes pas l'eau claire. Ainsi, dans ma fameuse mare de Vauroux, je vois des bêtes très drôles, très singulières; ça ressemble un peu à des mille-pattes, mais plus longs. . . . Un instant tu les verras flotter à la surface limpide de l'eau. Puis ils s'enfoncent tout à coup et, à leur place, monte un nuage de boue. Hé bien! ils nous ressemblent.[19]

But above all, it prefigures the most crucial episode in Donissan's own quest in "La Tentation du désespoir,"—which takes place, significantly, just before his encounter with her—in which, instead of reaching his destination, the village of Etaples where he is to hear confessions, he will be led round and round in the night by no one less than the Devil himself.

A close bond links the fatally hurt child whom we see turning into "a little servant of Satan, a Saint Brigid of the void,"[20] to the saint of Lumbres whose supernatural love finds in her its first prey and challenge. It is Mouchette's blind revolt after Cadignan's abuse of her and her fall into Satan's "silent, solitary, icy peace"[21] which seem to determine the saint's path. If he must venture more deeply than anyone after him into the Enemy's own domain, it is for

[19] *Ibid.*, p. 75.　　　[20] *Ibid.*, p. 220.　　　[21] *Ibid.*, p. 221.

her sake above all others. The enormous distance that separates Mouchette, who in her frailty has capsized almost immediately, from Donissan, who is advancing toward the Kingdom with giant strides, he must bridge, even at the price of perilous "returns," for his quest is inseparable from hers.

All the human and superhuman elements which are contained in the destiny of Mouchette we find enlarged and redeemed in Donissan's. She shares the violence of his passion, his boundless generosity and eagerness to give all without stopping to calculate the risks, his wrathful disappointment when the gift is abused and rejected, and, finally, his blind thirst, engendered by this wrath, to take revenge and annihilate the enemy, which will lead him very nearly, as it does her, into a state of satanic possession. But where she, in the blindness of her despair, persists in mistaking first the world, then herself, for the enemy and sets out to destroy others and herself with satanic hatred, the saint's vision, illuminated by love and hope, succeeds time and again in breaking through the same delusion and in uncovering the presence of the one who is the true adversary of the Father, his earth, and of all life.

In the opening part of "La Tentation du désespoir," Donissan seems indeed to bear a closer resemblance to the rebellious child than to a saint. Only the magnificent father figure of the Abbé Menou-Segrais stands between him and the abyss and saves him from shipwreck, for those countless others, headed by Mouchette, whom Donissan in turn has been destined to rescue. Whatever has been said about Bernanos' lack of concern with psychological elements seems very much open to question. In every one of the many instances of spiritual shipwreck he has depicted, in which a betrayed love of earth yields to the *vertige* of infinite nothingness, one notes the absence of a true father figure in the concrete, earthly configuration of characters. Invariably the Bernanosian victims of the false father's hatred of earth are orphans, at least in the psychological sense, whose dream of the Father's kingdom has never been released into full consciousness and allowed to become a true hope of redemption through the love and support of an earthly father. And conversely, we find by the side of every great protagonist the presence of a tender and vibrant father figure who launches and steers his child until the latter's vision of the goal is so clear that he can forge ahead by himself and trace his own path. As the Abbé Chevance launches Chantal de Clergerie in *La Joie*, so in "La Tentation du désespoir" the old Abbé Menou-Segrais watches in fear and trembling over the precious and vulnerable child that has been entrusted to him, as will the curé de Torcy over the young curé d'Ambricourt in the *Journal d'un curé de campagne*. Obviously Bernanos does not suggest that the presence or absence of this vital relationship of love and trust can fully account for his heroes' purity of vision or blind delusion. Such a reduction of the mystery of the spiritual life to its psychological components would be incompatible with a religious and poetic conception of life that is predicated above all else on God's freedom and on the fundamental flexibility and openness of the finite human situation in which this freedom continues to be an active force. Nevertheless, he does suggest that, in a world which satanic hatred keeps turning back into a sea of death, even the deepest source of grace cannot assure sustenance and hope unless the earthly vessel has discerned it clearly at least once through the loving reflection of a fellow quester's glance.

Only this kind of recognition by the Abbé Menou-Segrais, in the episode of the Christmas night, releases the deep hidden spring of the saint's life and sets him on his path. After years of arrest and exhausting efforts merely to keep afloat, we see him speeding ahead like a vessel with all its sails unfurled and heading straight for its destination:

> L'homme extraordinaire, que la défiance ou la pusillanimité de ses supérieurs avait renfermé des années dans un invisible réseau, trouvait enfin devant lui le champ libre, et s'y déployait. Chaque obstacle, abordé de front, pliait sous lui.[22]

He sets out "with the irresistible power of one who no longer calculates his chances" forging straight ahead. But already the element of death is awaiting him, to turn him back. It is seen alternately as the heaving sea itself, and, more touchingly, in the form of the sea's victim: the bleak landscape of a half-petrified, half-washed-out earth. From the beginning to the very end of Donissan's journey, we observe not only the sea—symbol of Satan's thirst—but also the earth itself, which the saint will spend his life blood to redeem and restore to life, halting his surging advance and turning it into an infernal circle. This movement comes into evidence first in his endless, exhausting, and seemingly futile rounds to the scattered farms of his parishioners:

> ... l'immense plaine ... tracée de chemins difficiles, balayée d'une bise aigre ... descend de la crête de la vallée ... à la mer. ... A travers l'herbe glacée qui glisse et cède sous les talons, il faut parfois cheminer longtemps pour trouver à la fin, au milieu d'un petit lac de boue creusé par les sabots des bêtes, une mauvaise barrière de bois qui grince et résiste entre ses montants pourris.[23]

His weariness grows until all he is conscious of is that the peasants eye him with suspicion and that his halting words rebound against their stubborn silence. His returns at night, in shame and bitterness, are the first signs of his Adversary's formidable power.

[22] *Ibid.*, p. 112.   [23] *Ibid.*, p. 114.

Quels retours, la nuit tombée, . . . lorsque l'amertume et la
honte est encore dans la bouche et que le coeur est seul, à
jamais![24]

Yet unlike Mouchette, or the many others who resemble
her for whom the first forced return means the end of the
journey, the saint's vision of the goal and his determination
to reach it revive and grow clearer with each defeat. The
miracle of the quest of a Donissan lies not in any success
visible to his own eyes in transforming the desert into a
flourishing land of fountains but in his emerging out of the
depth of each return into blind, despairing self-reflection
with clearer sight and more passionately thirsting for the
Father's kingdom than before. Against his ever-reborn and
strengthened will to resume his quest, even in the depths
of exhaustion, the Usurper is powerless. All the rounds that
we see Satan win against the intrepid peasant fail in the
end to add up to victory, because, in the decisive one in
which he has set the saint his most fatal snare, Donissan
defeats him.

The snare the Devil holds out for Donissan is the satanic
"double" of the greatest of God's gifts which the saint is
yet to receive, the gift of vision. Taking advantage of
Donissan's cruel doubts and disappointments and his bitter
thirst, Satan places before him an infinitely subtle and
transparent reflection of his innermost self and tempts him
with the power of self-knowledge. Donissan is overwhelmed.
But his inner vision of Paradise, though eclipsed at that
moment, is powerful enough to give the other the lie.
Dazzled though he is, he can still dimly discern that, for all
its uncanny penetration, the satanic vision is blindness.
It emanates from the hatred and thirst of the abyss and
can only seize on its own shadows, which it mistakes for
the substance of the living.

[24] *Ibid.*

Ce n'est pas *cela* dont j'ai besoin. . . . Que m'importe de me connaître? L'examen particulier, sans autre lumière suffit à un pauvre pécheur. Il parlait ainsi, bien que le regret de la vision perdue blessât toutes ses fibres. Le vertige d'une curiosité surnaturelle, désormais sans effet, à jamais, le laissait haletant, vide. Mais il croyait toucher au but.[25]

Donissan's heroic resistance breaks the snare. It sets free the divine glance of love by means of which he is destined, from that moment on, to free others more fragile than he from the deceitful mirror into which their being has been drawn and in which they are condemned to see the world as a hostile desert and themselves as its prisoners. But the price he has to pay for this victory is costly. The double the Devil has set before him in a moment of ineffable temptation has penetrated his consciousness and will, until the end of his tragic battle, mock him and seek to overshadow his every move, thought, and prayer.

The irony of his fate is most clearly manifest at the end of "La Tentation du désespoir." The very being for whose sake he has had to incur the curse of his double vision is the one whom he almost destroys because of it. Indeed, one is tempted to feel that he does destroy her and that for his blindness he has to accept the awful guilt of Mouchette's suicide before he can become the saint of Lumbres. The account of her conversion *in extremis* is not entirely convincing. It both detracts from the overwhelmingly real tragedy of the saint's own dereliction as he struggles to fulfill his superhuman vocation and tends to obscure the deepest link in his relationship to the girl—the risk, incurred by her as well as by him, that in slipping in the course of his dangerous descent to come to her rescue he may push her to her death.

[25] *Ibid.*, p. 176.

The scene in which Donissan at last comes upon Mouchette in the early dawn at the turn of the road where, demented by guilt and defiance, she awaits the appearance of her false hero whom she has shot, again unfolds in a circle. It opens out in a sweeping movement of love, as the saint's inner eye reaches out in a flash to the girl's wrecked and buried dream of Paradise; then rebounds sharply, suddenly leaving him faced not by the living and suffering human being before him but by a deserted hull which Satan has taken over. Throughout the first part of their strange meeting, we see his overflowing pity almost freeing Mouchette from the imprisoning posture of defiance in which she has blindly sought refuge. The tenderness of his voice and glance are reviving her like a pure spring of water, and her power of resistance is beginning to melt away:

> Et quand elle n'entendit plus en elle-même l'écho de cette voix dont la douceur l'avait transpercée, le regard paternel acheva de la confondre. Si paternel! . . . (Car il avait lui-même goûté le poison et savouré sa longue amertume.) . . . .[26]

As he talks to her and tries to make her see her guiltlessness in succumbing to the snare Satan set for her when she first set out in quest of love, as he shows her the Father's love that recognizes her by her longing and her struggle and not by the evil which the Other has wrought in her, his voice mingles with and draws back into her consciousness

> . . . le murmure déchirant de la conscience troublée dans sa source profonde, tellement que les deux voix ne faisaient plus qu'une plainte unique, comme un seul jet de sang vermeil.[27]

But the girl is too terrified to be able to relinquish the only support to which she has clung since her return, her pride. As he sees her face harden again, sees her bent on resisting him with her last, feeble energies, a blinding rage

[26] *Ibid.*, p. 199.   [27] *Ibid.*, pp. 203–4.

overcomes him. In a dramatic reversal, it is now the child's evil dream that we see pulling both into the satanic abyss:

> . . . les ténèbres étaient retombées. Pourquoi n'obéit-il pas alors au mouvement intérieur qui lui commandait de se dérober sans retard? Devant lui, ce n'était qu'une pauvre créature reformant en hâte la trame un instant déchirée de ses mensonges. . . . Mais n'avait-il pas été une minute—une éternité!—par un effort presque divin, affranchi de sa propre nature? Fut-ce le désespoir de cette puissance perdue? Ou la rage de la reconquérir? . . . Et déjà montait dans ses yeux la même lueur de lucidité surhumaine, cette fois dépouillée de toute pitié. Le don périlleux, il l'avait donc conquis de nouveau, par force, dans un élan désespéré, capable de faire violence, même au ciel. La grâce de Dieu s'était faite visible à ses yeux mortels: ils ne découvraient plus maintenant que l'ennemi, vautré dans sa proie. Et déjà aussi la pâle figure de Mouchette, comme rétrécie par l'angoisse, chavirait dans le même rêve, dont leur double regard échangeait le reflet hideux.[28]

A few hours later, Mouchette kills herself.

Once again, and for the last time, the Abbé Menou-Segrais saves Donissan from despair. With his deep perspicacity, he not only absolves Donissan from guilt in his far fall from grace, in which the Antagonist has avenged himself for the saint's triumph over him, but confirms him unhesitatingly in his path, despite the extraordinary risks this path entails.

> Sur la route que vous avez choisie—non! où vous vous êtes jeté!—vous serez seul, décidément seul, vous marcherez seul. Quiconque vous y suivrait, se perdrait sans vous secourir.[29]

In "Le Saint de Lumbres," the novel shifts to the last day of the saint's life, forty years later. The forty years suggest Christ's forty days in the desert. We see Donissan approaching the end of his journey, having spent himself

[28] *Ibid.*, pp. 206, 208.   [29] *Ibid.*, p. 242.

relentlessly in the struggle to revive through his love the wasteland of ennui, pride, avarice and lust into which satanic thirst has thrust his children. The evocation of this last day and of the final brutal test to which he is put, and which he fails, is dominated by the same satanic motif which is present in both the "Prologue" and "La Tentation du désespoir," to the point of overshadowing even the latter part's great opening moment of hope and expectancy, the Christmas night. At the very moment of fulfillment, when the saint's prophetic vision has become for thousands an unfailing beacon they follow with trust and love, he himself is once again blinded and unable to discern the enormous distance he and his own have covered in their journey.

In the most brutal assault of despair he has ever suffered, the world of men he has loved so passionately is eclipsed before his eyes. All he can see around him is a desert in which his consuming labors have failed to bring even the smallest corner to life; and, in the corresponding image, an untamed ocean filled with human wreckage in which, in the course of forty years, he has simply been tossed about, to end up exactly where he started. In the satanic mirror his tired gaze cannot resist, he sees himself as a captive of the very vessels he has been leading, pulled by them into the infernal circle of hopeful launchings, violent arrests, and despairing returns to chaos from which he has struggled to extricate them.

> Aujourd'hui comme hier, comme au premier jour . . . les mêmes. . . . Il est au terme de son effort, et l'obstacle manque tout à coup. Ceux qu'il a voulu délivrer, c'étaient ceux-là mêmes qui refusent la liberté comme un fardeau, et l'ennemi qu'il a poursuivi jusqu'au ciel rit au-dessous, insaisissable, invulnérable.[30]

[30] *Ibid.*, p. 254.

On the edge of despair, the saint's glance turns into a withering gaze of contempt for the earth, and his sublime dream of the Father's land of fountains into a satanic dream of water:

Il ne voit derrière lui qu'un paysage aride, et ces foules qu'il a traversées, en les bénissant. Mais quoi! Le troupeau trotte encore sur ses talons, le poursuit, le presse, ne lui laisse aucun repos, insatiable. . . . Non! il ne tournera pas la tête, il ne veut pas. Ils l'ont poussé jusqu-là, jusqu'au bord, et au-delà . . . ô miracle! il y a le silence, le vrai silence, l'incomparable silence, son repos.—Mourir, dit-il à voix basse, mourir. . . . il est à cette minute où Satan pèse de tout son poids, où s'appliquent au même point, d'une seule pesée, toutes les puissance d'en bas.[31]

Only the saint's will which, through his numberless trials has become as hard and unshakable as a rock, makes him hold out once again against the heaving upsurge of the satanic water. But again, and for the last time, he must pay for its massive strength with a crushing defeat. In the last round of Donissan's battle with Satan, in which the Antagonist is stripped of all disguises and becomes one with death, the saint is not destroyed in the ultimate sense. We see him emerging from it, as from all previous defeats, further than ever from surrender, and more wrathfully defiant. But this final defeat, in which he is cursed to see the defeat of life itself, and of the Father who is the source of all life, at the hands of death and its Master, breaks his heart.

The episode starts magnificently. We see the old man freed by an urgent signal of distress from the satanic mirage of peace and silence that has encircled him. A father is waiting in despair to take Donissan to a dying child.

[31] *Ibid.*, pp. 257–58.

Instantaneously, the circle gives way to a clear, open path, and the monotonous desert of evil to the vibrant world of living beings:

> Par la mince fissure, le réel glisse et rejaillit, reprend son niveau. Un signe nous rappelle, un mot tout bas murmuré ressuscite un monde aboli, et tel parfum jadis respiré est plus tenace que la mort. . . . Un malade, un de ses enfants! . . . Toute la petite paroisse, et tant d'âmes à travers le monde, dont il était la force et la joie, l'appellent, le nomment. . . . Il écoute; il a déjà répondu; il est prêt.[32]

But the challenge which awaits him is superhuman. The child has died; and the mother in her boundless faith in his miracle-working powers is expecting him to bring the boy back to life. As the episode unfolds, it recapitulates and sums up the fundamental tragedy of the rebel-saint of Lumbres. Cursed to the depths of his being by his satanic double, which contests and threatens to overshadow the purest, most inspired promptings of his soul, Donissan mistakes the clear inner voice telling him to save the child for a satanic temptation. Able to see only the absurd discrepancy between the superhuman act he is called upon to perform and his own blindness and indignity, he is unable to trust the promise that has clearly been given him and lets the moment of grace pass by. But no sooner has he forfeited it, than he realizes that he has again been duped by his double. In the dramatic climax of the episode, the mother sees not a saint but a wrathful warrior storming into the room where the dead child is lying, no longer with any hope of saving the child but with a blind determination to wrench out of the satanic jaw the prey of which he has been cheated.

> Elle s'avance vers lui, s'arrête, frappée jusque dans son espérance à la vue de ce visage altéré, où elle ne lit qu'une volonté farouche, visage de héros, non de saint.[33]

[32] *Ibid.*, p. 259.   [33] *Ibid.*, p. 298.

No longer focused on the divine promise that alone could restore the dead child to life, Donissan's hate-filled glance pierces its object and slips right through it into the infinitely elusive and mocking eye of the Adversary.

First, we see the dead child in the beautiful, characteristic image of a little ship that has been pulled up short:

Le lit de fer, avec son froid petit fardeau, ressemble à un merveilleux navire, qui a jeté l'ancre pour toujours.[34]

But as Donissan gazes at the dead boy's face and in a superhuman effort of pure, defiant will directed against the Enemy almost accomplishes the miracle of prying the boy loose and bringing him back to life, a satanic gleam of triumphant irony pierces him through the child's half-opened eyes:

Et voici que le mort l'a devancé: *c'est lui qui l'attend*, pareil à un adversaire résolu, sur ses gardes. . . . Les prunelles, d'un mat noir, n'ont plus de pensée humaine. . . . Et pourtant. . . . Une autre pensée peut-être? . . . Une ironie bientôt reconnue, dans un éclair. . . . Le défi du maître de la mort, du voleur d'hommes. . . . C'est lui.[35]

Not only does death snatch the child from him again, but for his last reckless attack on the Prince of death, Donissan pays with his own life. Through the symbolic transformation of the curse which he has borne to the end into the heart pain of angina pectoris, Bernanos vindicates his extraordinary saint even in his deepest defeat. As Donissan drags himself back home, dazed by pain, his return suggests not his own betrayal of his goal but his defeat by the Father's own unconquerable Enemy.

Qu'elle est longue la route du retour, la longue route! Celle des armées battues, la route du soir, qui ne mène à rien, dans la poussière vaine. . . ![36]

[34] *Ibid.*, p. 300.   [35] *Ibid.*   [36] *Ibid.*, p. 311.

Up to his last terrible hour, in which the pain virtually divides him in two—into the empty, broken hull of an "old athlete, pierced by a thousand blows" and the transparent spring of love which, mysteriously, keeps on flowing through the wreckage—Donissan testifies to the Father on behalf of the human earth's invincible dream of Paradise:

> C'est par son cri de douleur que s'exprime la race humaine, la plainte arrachée à ses flancs par un effort démesuré. Vous nous avez jetés dans l'épaisseur comme un levain. L'univers que le péché nous a ôté, nous le reprendrons pouce par pouce, nous vous le rendrons tel que nous le reçûmes, dans son ordre et sa sainteté, au premier matin des jours.[37]

[37] *Ibid.*, p. 362.

> Chaque vie de saint est comme une nouvelle floraison, l'effusion dans le monde rendu, par l'hérédité du péché, esclave de ses morts—d'une miraculeuse, d'une édénique ingénuité.
>
> Saint Dominique
>
> C'etait un mince filet d'eau limpide, et maintenant cela déborde de l'âme, me remplit de fraîcheur.
>
> Journal d'un curé de campagne

VI.

The Land of Fountains

Only nine years separate *Sous le Soleil de Satan*, and its abrupt shifts from blissful visions of the azure gulf of the Father's love to blind satanic thirst, from Bernanos' purest and most songful Magnificat, the *Journal d'un curé de campagne*. In the Bernanosian landscape, the *Journal* emerges as an oasis, halfway between the rocky desert of *L'Imposture* and the heaving satanic waters of *Monsieur Ouine*. It marks that miraculous moment in the Bernanosian quest for Paradise at which, for once, we see the distant Paradise become an earthly reality, at which, in the curé d'Ambricourt's last words, "everything is grace."[1]

For once and once only, the Bernanosian imagination has succeeded in freeing the finite, earthly landscape of human endeavor from the encroachment of the satanic water by purging the springs of the earth to the point where even the poorest soil can taste the promise of redemption. All of

---

[1] *Journal d'un curé de campagne*, p. 336.

the writer's love of earth is released in this masterpiece of faith and artistic maturity. That love prevails at last both over the impatience of the vessels of grace of his earlier works to leave behind the "place of exile" and enter the eternal Kingdom and over his rebels' despair of earth's poverty and corruption and the *vertige* induced in them by the waters of death. In the *Journal*, the earth is no longer conceived as a more or less passive battleground, pawn in a wholly supernatural battle between the transcendent forces of divine love and satanic hatred. It moves to the foreground of the drama as a major participant in its own right.

The unique significance of the *Journal* in Bernanos' evolution both as an artist and a Christian lies in this, that throughout its pages we see a curse lifted from the earth. The earth's thirst for the infinite is no longer seen as so incommensurable with the resources of its own inner springs of life that it must almost inevitably succumb to the satanic delusion of plenitude, as held out by the sea, or be delivered from the agony of its finiteness in mystic ecstasy. Slowly the image of the somber Garden of Olives in which the protagonist is exiled and assumes his part in the redemptive Passion of Christ is enlarged by a wholly new dimension. The mystery of the Incarnation begins to cast a light of its own, in which the earth is displayed not as humiliated but as triumphant in its very poverty. Chosen by the infinite divine spirit as a partner and co-creator, the earth invites and makes possible God's most beautiful and unpredictable inspirations. In the *Journal*, the earth's immense role in the drama of creation that is steadily unfolding through time at last becomes fully visible: it is seen as nothing less than the challenger and embodiment of the creative spirit at work, the precious clay in which the finite and the transcendent, time and eternity, earth and water, are reconciled and become one in a positive, dynamic union.

By surrounding his young dreamer, the curé d'Ambricourt, with some of the most moving and noble "earth" figures of his creation—the curé de Torcy, representative of the rich and fertile soil of Flanders, the countess, Doctor Delbende, Olivier de Mainville—Bernanos does more than vindicate the essential beauty and nobility of the human landscape which through most of his works we see ravaged beyond hope by the satanic flood. Through that landscape he anchors the curé d'Ambricourt's ardent dream of Paradise in the solid realm of the here and now and saves him from the dreamer's *vertige* of water.

The young priest's first glimpse of his forlorn parish of Ambricourt is well designed to overwhelm him. Virtually all of Ambricourt has succumbed to the images of Satan's vast mirror of delusion, in which the earth is reflected as a paradise of self-sufficient splendor, while in reality it is slowly being smothered under alternate layers of dust and rain—symbols of satanic ennui. Its false dream has, through the generations, given the whole parish that aloof and predatory character against which no exertion of love seems able to prevail. From the count to the poorest peasants, each seeks to escape from the challenge of his existence—to become a man in the full sense of the word by reaching through his own finite being the divine source of life—and prefers instead to barricade himself within the illusory security of material wealth. Time and again, the curé d'Ambricourt sees himself reduced to impotence by the blight that the delusion of plenty has caused all around him. All he can do is watch and pray in terror as death uncovers in one after another of the self-satisfied notaries and tradesmen of Ambricourt the scornful hoax through which Satan has cheated them of their true richness and of life.

Je crois, je suis sûr [he reflects] que beaucoup d'hommes n'engagent jamais leur être, leur sincérité profonde. Ils vivent à la surface d'eux-mêmes, et le sol humain est si riche que cette mince couche superficielle suffit pour une maigre moisson, qui donne l'illusion d'une véritable destinée. . . . Combien d'hommes n'auront jamais la moindre idée de l'héroisme surnaturel, sans quoi il n'est pas de vie intérieure! Et c'est justement sur cette vie-là qu'ils seront jugés: dès qu'on y réfléchit un peu, la chose paraît certaine, évidente. Alors? . . . Alors dépouillés par la mort de tous ces membres artificiels que la société fournit aux gens de leur espèce, ils se retrouveront tels qu'ils sont, qu'ils étaient à leur insu— d'affreux monstres non développés, des moignons d'hommes.[2]

His passionate endeavors to break through the rigid armor of earthly props appear to be nullified, just like Donissan's, by the resistance of a soil already too benumbed by the spreading cancer of greed to respond to the promise of true abundance with anything but abject fear. It is either so encrusted in pride and mistrust to respond to him at all, or else it crumbles at his slightest touch with self-pity and induces in him a *dégoût* that nearly overwhelms him:

La personne humaine aura été lentement rongée, comme une poutre par ces champignons invisibles qui, en quelques semaines, font d'une pièce de chêne une matière spongieuse que le doigt crève sans effort.[3]

To be able to cure the soil entrusted to him of its rot would demand that some part of it, somewhere, still be whole and healthy; but for a while all he can see is a humanity that appears to have lost its fundamental natural properties of courage, generosity, and sense of justice, to a point where grace finds literally nothing left to redeem.

Le mal jeté n'importe où, germe presque sûrement, [he reflects despairingly]. Au lieu qu'il faut à la moindre semence de bien, pour ne pas être étouffée, une chance extraordinaire, un prodigieux bonheur.[4]

[2] *Ibid.*, p. 135.   [3] *Ibid.*, p. 179.   [4] *Ibid.*, p. 128.

Repeatedly through the first half of the *Journal*, we see his glance slipping off the unsubstantial reality before him and, lacking all firm support, gliding back into the "night" of the satanic sea:

> Rien. Dieu! je respire, j'aspire la nuit, la nuit entre en moi par je ne sais quelle inconcevable brêche de l'âme. Je suis moi-même nuit. . . . Il me semble avoir fait à rebours tout le chemin parcouru depuis que Dieu m'a tiré de rien.[5]

However, in contrast to Chantal's or Donissan's unmitigated sense of exile, of being abandoned for the duration of their earthly existence in a realm in which Satan has virtually triumphed and which, it would appear, can be saved only *in extremis* at the end of time, Ambricourt places before Bernanos' most beloved dreamer a challenge that vibrantly reconfirms his faith in the earth's salvation and reopens his eyes to its hidden treasures. Significantly, the *Journal's* turning point is the joyful moment which emerges out of one of his most devastating seizures of *vertige*, when the curé d'Ambricourt is able to free and bring to a true, though belated, flowering the life of Ambricourt's noblest creature, the countess.

Victim of an excess of earthly pride, the countess is a figure of heroic stature. On the natural level the complete opposite of him in her almost crushing wealth of will and wordly assurance, she is yet able to meet him and the challenge he holds out to her on a level that is worthy of his own sublime poverty. Just as for him, dispossessed orphan of earth and dreamer of an unearthly Paradise, so for her, heiress to a long and proud worldly heritage, life cannot be a cautious maneuver for survival. It is a wager on which she has staked all she has, to win all or lose all. Unlike her corrupt husband, who exploits others at the

---

[5] *Ibid.*, pp. 132–33.

least possible risk and cost to himself, the countess is a beautiful embodiment of that passion for earthly justice which, in the Bernanosian vision, is one of the most fertile grounds for hope in the divine justice of the Father. Heading the roster of less fully developed kindred characters— Doctor Delbende, her daughter Chantal, and her nephew, Olivier de Mainville—she is a representative of the few authentically proud and noble beings who come right after Bernanos' saints in keeping alive the artist's hope for the human race and for the earth it holds in trust. Her role in the destiny of the curé d'Ambricourt is immense, for, together with them, she is instrumental in saving him from despair.

The significant thing to note about Bernanos' conception of the countess and of her role in the *Journal*, which may shed a good deal of light on the conception of the whole work, is that while she may possibly be an intrinsically nobler and more solid figure than his earlier rebels she is above all a more authentically earthbound one. The satanic force that has taken hold of her does not "possess" her as it does them, to the point where we see her deprived of her purely human, earthly dimension altogether. What remains in the foreground of her tragedy is the earthly basis of her satanic defiance of God; namely, her loving and noble heart's grief over the loss of her infant son and its outrage in face of a divine will that can thus violate man's sense of justice. And curiously, in conceiving her not as a "satanic" figure but on a less absolute plane, as a majestic figure of human suffering and human revolt whose thirst for justice cries to heaven, Bernanos adds to rather than detracts from her stature, and weights the odds against her, and against grace in its battle for her, less heavily. An element of freedom is brought to light, whereby the earth itself, as embodied in her, asserts itself actively and through which the center of gravity of the Bernanosian drama of salvation is shifted from the divine-satanic contest of the two waters, unleashed by the Fall, to the divine-human labor of redemption made possible by the Incarnation.

The great beauty and fruitfulness of the crucial encounter that takes place between the countess and the curé d'Ambricourt, in which not only she—embodiment of earth—is reconciled to the will of the Father but he, the heroic dreamer of the infinite, is reconciled to the earth's and his own agonizing finiteness and privation, stems perhaps from this alone, that the ground on which the two first meet is that of an elemental human sorrow. In its compelling concreteness and universality, sorrow creates a link between the two that releases in both springs of love unlike any to be found in analogous episodes in the earlier works. In their confrontation, Bernanos has gone beyond the abstract and largely symbolic conception of characters which underlies works like *L'Imposture*, to give only one example, whose Cénabre and Chevance are magnified beyond their human dimensions to the point where they become almost pure embodiments and extensions of satanic defiance and divine grace. No earthly communion really seems possible between the ominous, giant rock, Cénabre, and the humble and tearful Abbé Chevance. They can meet only in eternity. In contrast, the central episode in *Journal* which turns the tide of two destinies is a superficially less dramatic but actually much more completely realized and far-reaching exchange between two fully individualized figures who, before they recognize each other as victim or emissary of a transcendent order, are drawn together by a shared suffering that is wholly of this earth.

Before the countess has even the first intimation of the magnitude of the curé d'Ambricourt's redemptive vocation, her pity goes out to him in his physical wretchedness as a mother's to a sick child. Her earthbound strength bolsters his own faltering courage; her noble face and bearing fill his heart to overflowing with reverence. Before she becomes his child in the sense of accepting his spiritual paternity, she is a mother who strengthens his fragile bonds with the earth. To the orphaned and lonely dreamer who, from the earliest years of his miserable life which he spent crouched behind the counter of his aunt's filthy tavern, has seen men turned into beasts by cruelty and lust, who has tasted despair, "the devil's richest elixir—his ambrosia,"[6] she is a precious and desperately needed reminder of the fundamental majesty of human beings. To her in turn, his frailty and his marvelous directness and innocence are reminders of the son whom she has lost. His innocence, which contrasts so dramatically with the calculating selfishness of the people among whom she must spend her life, disarms her pride. Nowhere else has Bernanos prepared the ground for the reconciliation of earth and spirit with greater love. The movement in which the episode unfolds is characteristic of the entire work. It begins as a concrete, earthbound confrontation in which both partners face together the depth of their human destitution; then opens out magnificently in height and depth as both are led to discover at the bottom not the thirsty water of the abyss but the most hidden and unsuspected springs of love.

The curé d'Ambricourt initiates this movement when he warns the countess, timidly but firmly, that Chantal may be on the verge of suicide. Stung to the quick, the proud woman who for years has set all her pride on being a model of virtue and resignation drops her dignified reserve and lets the hatred that has been poisoning her heart surge over him like an evil flood. He is stunned by its impact:

[6] *Ibid.*, p. 137.

Mon Dieu, est-ce à cause du désordre de ma pensée, de mon coeur?—L'angoisse dont je souffre est-elle contagieuse? J'ai, depuis quelque temps, l'impression que ma seule présence fait sortir le péché de son repaire, l'amène comme à la surface de l'être, dans les yeux, la bouche, la voix. . . . On dirait que l'ennemi dédaigne de rester caché devant un si chétif adversaire, vient me défier en face, se rit de moi.[7]

The bitterness that pours out of her—against her family, her life, finally against God—awakens powerfully all the revolt that since his childhood has kept flaring up in his own heart at the sight of human misery. Summoning all his strength, he warns her—and in a sense himself—against a defiance that can only remove her further from the dead child and from all that she has ever loved and longed for. He makes her see how far it has already separated her from the living, especially from the child who remains to her and needs her, and has turned her into one of those impenetrable rocks that eventually nothing may be able to reach:

Le malheur, l'inconcevable malheur de ces pierres embrasées qui furent des hommes c'est qu'elles n'ont plus rien à partager.[8]

He is so emptied of all hope and strength himself at that moment and in such intense physical pain, that only his magnificent fidelity to his calling, his unconditional readiness to "face up" to her imperious cry for justice despite his "empty hands," saves both from the abyss. But this fidelity itself proves to have irresistible force. From the deepest recesses of his being, it calls up the grace that restores first him then the countess to life:

C'est alors—non! cela ne peut s'exprimer—tandis que je luttais de toutes mes forces contre le doute, la peur, que l'esprit de prière rentra en moi. Qu'on m'entende bien: depuis le début de cet entretien extraordinaire, je n'avais

---

[7] *Ibid.*, pp. 188–89.　　[8] *Ibia.*, p. 201.

cessé de prier, au sens que les chrétiens frivoles donnent à ce mot. Une malheureuse bête, sous la cloche pneumatique, peut faire tous les mouvements de la respiration, qu'importe! Et voilà que soudain, l'air siffle de nouveau dans ses bronches déplie un à un les delicats tissus pulmonaires, déjà flétris, les artères tremblent au premier coup de bélier du sang rouge— l'être entier est comme un navire à la détonation des voiles qui se gonflent.[9]

In a flawless transition, we see the current of grace take over at the exact limit of his human endurance and free both of the mesmerizing reflections of despair. Addressing himself now to her submerged love alone, he is able to make her see the truth: not the child's death but only her proud delusion that she can keep his presence alive in her heart while defying God will separate her from the boy forever.

Tant que nous sommes en vie [he tells her], nous pouvons nous faire illusion, croire que nous aimons par nos propres forces, que nous aimons hors de Dieu. Mais nous ressemblons à des fous qui tendent les bras vers le reflet de la lune dans l'eau.[10]

The countess' response is striking in its wholeness. Above all other rebels whom we see the Bernanosian protagonists struggling to wrench out of their armor of defiance, she represents an earth so deeply imbued with the promise of redemption that, the moment the shock of truth pierces her, she is as heroic in facing and accepting it as she was before in serving her delusion. As she lets his insight reopen her deep wound and struggles valiantly to master her pride that has for so long kept her in a state of death and immunity from pain, the curé d'Ambricourt has the blissful feeling that they have both been released from exile:

Je ne perdais aucun de ses mouvements, et cependant j'avais l'impression étrange que nous n'étions ni l'un ni l'autre dans ce triste petit salon, que la pièce était vide.[11]

[9] *Ibid.*, p. 207.   [10] *Ibid.*, p. 210.   [11] *Ibid.*, p. 207.

The space that opens up all around them transcends the narrow boundaries of earthly life. It is the Kingdom of God, which encompasses the living and the dead and in which all earthly love is brought to fruition by the infinite "azure gulf" that it discovers it has borne all along in its own depth.

> Il me semblait [the curé d'Ambricourt writes of that moment] qu'une main mystérieuse venait d'ouvrir une brèche dans on ne sait quelle muraille invisible, et la paix rentrait de toutes parts, prenait majestueusement son niveau, une paix inconnue de la terre, la douce paix des morts, ainsi qu'une eau profonde.[12]

The reconciliation which takes place here between water and earth is so complete that it not only frees the countess from her hell of hatred but preserves the curé d'Ambricourt from the curse through which Bernanos' earlier protagonists receive in exchange for their outflowing grace their partner's blind despair. Here the mystic exchange is grounded so solidly in an earthly communion that no degree of exhaustion can make him lose his footing. The grace he has been able to make accessible to her flows back through him in an infinitely gentle movement that forestalls the fatal recoil. It anchors him, on the contrary, more deeply in the vibrant hope of seeing the earth freed from the Enemy's gaze and restored to the Father:

> La paix que j'avais appelée sur elle était descendue sur moi. Et si simple, si familière qu'aucune présence n'aurait pu réussir à la troubler. Oui, nous étions rentrés si doucement dans la vie de chaque jour que le témoin le plus attentif n'eût rien surpris de ce secret, qui déjà ne nous appartenait plus.[13]

The beautiful simplicity and sobriety of this episode, characteristic of the entire *Journal*, the perfect containment

[12] *Ibid.*, p. 208.   [13] *Ibid.*, p. 212.

of its supernatural dimensions within the confines of a humble and inconspicuous setting, is more than an artistic accomplishment. It is also the clue to the clearly visible success which sets the quest of the curé d'Ambricourt for Paradise apart from that of all his predecessors along the same journey. Alone among all of them, he is not only called to share the Agony of Christ's abandonment in the Garden of Olives but is able, in the end, to taste the joy of his own redemption by seeing himself freed from the satanic shadow that has pursued him throughout most of his path. What Donissan was unable to bring about by superhuman exertions, the curé d'Ambricourt is able to accomplish because, in the course of the arduous apprenticeship we see him undergoing in the *Journal*, he learns to let the inherent redemptive power of his own earthbound poverty come into full play and fight on his side. The *Journal* is, both from an artistic and a religious point of view, Bernanos' truest celebration of poverty. Through its pages, the very finiteness of earth becomes both the protagonist's most reliable support against the magic of the satanic water and eventually his infallible gateway to the infinite "azure gulf."

The work's diary form itself suggests the dominant dimension of *Journal*. The principal purpose of the curé d'Ambricourt's diary, as he himself conceives it, is to free him from the blinding *vertige* of the infinite that threatens to divorce him from earth. It is to summon him back to the concrete, humble reality of his own existence each time that the unmeasured *élan* of his dream of Paradise makes him lose his footing and threatens to cast him back into the sea of death. For the first time in a Bernanosian work, we see the protagonist's glance deliberately turning on himself not in self-delusion but in the heroic endeavor to face up fully to his own finite share in the divine work of redemption and to see it as clearly as possible. The challenge this fragile dreamer sets for himself, as he records his daily, hourly battles against his own terrors and "hateful weakness" and against the myriad delusions of richness that he sees throttling his flock, is indeed a complex and heroic one. It is to learn to accept the poverty of his condition, which has filled him with both pain and shame, and to turn it into the royal poverty of one who is conscious that, while nothing that he has or does can of itself bear fruit, it is through his "empty hands" that the Father has chosen to complete his work of creation. It is a challenge fit for a king, for if he fails to do his part, grace itself suffers a setback.

> . . . que pèsent nos chances à nous autres [he wonders, as the diary holds out to him the temptation of seeking refuge in delusion] qui avons accepté, une fois pour toutes, l'effrayante présence du divin à chaque instant de notre pauvre vie. . . ! Calculer nos chances, à quoi bon? On ne joue pas contre Dieu.[14]

A poverty thus conceived becomes the greatest human achievement possible for the Bernanosian dreamer of Paradise. It demands not only that he abandon himself without hesitation to the least current of grace, lest he forfeit its benefit, but above all that he be ready and sturdy enough, when turned back upon himself, to resist the vertiginous appeal of the sea that promises infinity and to remain true to himself and the Father by plowing more deeply into his humble earthly resources of endurance, lucid courage, and fidelity until a new spring is released and grace flows again.

> Riches ou pauvres, regardez-vous donc plutôt dans la pauvreté comme dans un miroir car elle est l'image de votre déception fondamentale, elle garde ici-bas la place du Paradis perdu, elle est le vide de vos coeurs, de vos mains.[15]

[14] *Ibid.*, p. 7.   [15] *Ibid.*, pp. 79–80.

The danger attendant on the curé d'Ambricourt's determination to realize his dream not by circumventing his own
finite, deficient being, which fills him with loathing, but on
the contrary by probing its depths is immediately apparent
in the diary's first pages. No sooner has he sat down to
write his first entry in the plain notebook than an instinctive
terror warns him that he is calling up not himself but
"another." This "other" is the fluid dream-image of himself held out to him by the satanic water, which, instead of
consolidating them, threatens to dissolve all the fibers of
his soul:

> Lorsque je me suis assis pour la première fois devant ce
> cahier d'écolier, j'ai tâché de fixer mon attention, de me
> recueillir comme pour un examen de conscience. Mais ce
> n'est pas ma conscience que j'ai vue de ce regard intérieur
> ordinairement si calme, si pénétrant, qui néglige le détail, va
> d'emblée à l'essentiel. Il semblait glisser à la surface d'une
> autre conscience jusqu'alors inconnue de moi, d'un miroir
> trouble où j'ai craint tout à coup de voir surgir un visage—
> quel visage: le mien peut-être . . . ? Un visage retrouvé,
> oublié. Il faudrait parler de soi avec une rigueur inflexible.
> Et au premier effort pour me saisir, d'ou viennent cette
> pitié, cette tendresse, ce relâchement de toutes les fibres de
> l'âme et cette envie de pleurer?[16]

But the dissolving satanic double that is the special curse
of the dreamer and that the diary is drawing to the surface
is met by powerful forces. They are, first of all, the curé
d'Ambricourt's own humility and superb natural pride,
preserving him from self-deception, and secondly, the vig-
orous down-to-earth tutelage of his mentor, the curé de
Torcy, who helps him to keep his feet and focus his attention firmly on the ground.

> Ta prière s'écoule en rêve [he tells him sternly]. Rien de plus
> grave pour l'âme que cette hémorragie-là![17]

[16] *Ibid.*, p. 9.   [17] *Ibid.*, p. 248.

The curé de Torcy is an exceptional figure among Bernanos' vessels of grace. Whereas Chevance, Chantal, and the curé d'Ambricourt himself are essentially unearthly creatures who feel truly at home only in the depths of their mystical vision, in which the soul is released from its earthly bonds, and to whom the earth remains an obstacle to overcome, the curé de Torcy is, as perhaps only Constance and Mère Lidoine in the *Dialogues des Carmélites* besides him, and they on a smaller scale, a superb embodiment of nature ennobled by grace. No corruption, no stench, no flood of sorrow, can overwhelm him because he knows them to be an integral part of earthly existence, and nothing earthly is alien to him. His is the humbler share in the great drama of salvation—not "David's harp" but the daily, repeated cleaning of the stable and the binding up of wounds in the "zoo" his mocking and loving glance conceives the human race to be. Like the rich soil of Flanders which has produced him, which resists both drought and flood, the curé de Torcy is royal in his plainness. Though he is devoid of the mystical *élan* of Bernanos' great dreamers, his glance has an unalterable purity nothing can corrupt. Underneath his deepest sorrow, "his soul is gay,"[18] the inner spring of hope remains untainted. The curé d'Ambricourt reflects on the mysterious vibrancy of his voice:

> Elle a beau être grave, on ne peut pas dire qu'elle soit triste: elle garde un certain frémissement presque imperceptible qui est comme la joie intérieure, une joie si profonde que rien ne saurait l'altérer, comme ces grandes eaux calmes, au-dessous des tempêtes.[19]

In the curé de Torcy, the very perfection of the purely human qualities of humility, courage, and constancy calls forth so sustained a flow of grace that he emerges as a figure

[18] *Ibid.*, p. 26.   [19] *Ibid.*, pp. 143–44.

of "supernatural power." His resolute earthliness in his Father's service has the force of an unflinching, irresistible supplication to which the Father cannot but respond. "This is how a king might beg," the curé d'Ambricourt notes in his diary, after seeing his master in one of the latter's deepest moments of anguish, shortly after his friend, Dr. Delbende, has committed suicide.

> Son visage laisse voir sa souffrance, l'exprime avec une franchise, une simplicité vraiment souveraines. En de telles conjonctures, il arrive de surprendre chez les meilleurs un regard équivoque, de ces regards qui disent plus ou moins clairement: "Vous voyez, je tiens bon, ne me louez pas, cela m'est naturel, merci. . . ." Le sien cherche naïvement votre compassion, votre sympathie, mais avec une noblesse! Ainsi pourrait mendier un roi.[20]

From the first, the curé de Torcy discerns the danger which threatens the pale-faced, "romantic" boy God has placed under his wing and proceeds vigorously to bolster him against it. It is under his tutelage that the curé d'Ambricourt learns to steady his glance, each time that it is diverted from earthly reality by an excess of revolt or exhaustion, by concentrating it on immediate, humble tasks commensurate with his strength. His apprenticeship is clearly modeled on the "little way" of Saint Thérèse of Lisieux. The Little Flower's impact on the Bernanosian imagination can hardly be overestimated. More than any other saint it is she, certainly, who helped the writer overcome the *vertige* of death, born of his *vertige* of the infinite, and who, through the curé de Torcy, saves the curé d'Ambricourt from the satanic eye of the sea:

> "Apporter de la paille fraîche au boeuf, étriller l'âne," ces paroles me sont revenues ce matin tandis que je pelais mes pommes de terre pour la soupe.[21]

[20] *Ibid.*, p. 139.   [21] *Ibid.*, p. 26.

In the many moments when he feels paralyzed by the apparent hopelessness of trying to wrench some of his poor and oppressed flock—whose wretchedness he himself has known all too well—out of the delusion which promises them a false paradise on earth, these words of the curé de Torcy come to his rescue. Very gently, they draw his glance out of the supernatural realm of the fallen Angel's power and into a concrete situation and a specific moment of time which demand of him only what he has the strength to give. They remind him that there is a time for surging advances and a time for patiently repairing the disorder wrought by the Devil in the night, "which belongs to him."[22]

> Travaille [his mentor exhorts him] . . . fais des petites choses, en attendant au jour le jour. . . . Voilà comment le bon Dieu souhaite nous voir, lorsqu'il nous abandonne à nos propres forces. Les petites choses n'ont l'air de rien, mais elles donnent la paix. C'est comme les fleurs des champs, vois-tu. On les croit sans parfum, et toutes ensemble, elles embaument.[23]

Under the tempering influence of the "little way," the curé d'Ambricourt's passionate revolt against the injustices he finds rampant all around him is preserved from the curse of blind despair which, in the life of one of the *Journal's* great rebels, Dr. Delbende, has become tantamount to a rebellion against life itself and has thrown him straight into the Enemy's jaws. Gradually the curé learns to confine his battle to the limits of a human, not an angelic revolt, commensurate with his limited resources, and becomes less vulnerable to the snare, of which the curé de Torcy has warned him, that Satan sets for those who let the sight of injustice overwhelm them:

[22] *Ibid.*, p. 14.   [23] *Ibid.*, p. 255.

Il ne faut pas que tu te laisses dévorer. Surtout ne va pas croire que tu la ferais reculer en la fixant dans les yeux comme un dompteur! Tu n'échapperas pas à sa fascination, à son vertige. Ne la regarde que juste ce qu'il faut, et ne la regarde jamais sans prier.[24]

As the diary places before his eyes the endless succession of grinding chores and large and small tribulations and joys of which, to his astonishment, his life seems to be made up, it offers him one of the deepest insights into the redemptive aspect of his finiteness or poverty. He is able to see that his inability to focus his attention clearly on anything except the pressing challenge of the moment is in itself a grace, that it is helping to keep his glance free both from the blinding snare of impossible, timeless absolutes and from the mesmerizing reflections of memory and anticipation into which satanic ennui insinuates itself and which only serve to eclipse the reality of the present moment. All that is ever given him is the fugitive present moment and the strength to face it as it comes. One of the most poignant examples of this is his realization, only hours after he has restored the countess to life, that already that joy, one of the deepest ever granted him, is fading from his consciousness:

C'est une joie sans visage. Ce qui devrait être, a été, n'est déjà plus, voilà tout.[25]

Every moment flashing into his consciousness, pregnant with its own unique demands and gifts, is met by the total, concentrated response of his attention, strength and love, and makes way immediately for the following one. Gradually, as the diary unfolds, a superb continuity develops in the course of the curé d'Ambricourt's journey, in which he advances from his first stumbling steps in his old, joyless

24 *Ibid.*, p. 76.   25 *Ibid.*, p. 213.

parish to the death that marks his coming into the full inheritance of the Father's Kingdom and its eternal, youthful joy of mornings in which "everything is beginning, and never ceases to begin."[26] A rhythm is established in his life between dryness and overflowing abundance, sorrow and joy, which becomes almost organic, suggesting the alternation of seasons. Slowly we see him evolving into a figure in whom grace and nature meet in a flawless continuity which in the end makes possible the greatest of miracles, the reconciliation of his dream with the tragic reality of his suffering, finite self:

> L'espèce de méfiance que j'avais de moi, de ma personne [he writes in his last pages], vient de se dissiper, je crois, pour toujours. . . . Je suis réconcilié avec moi-même, avec cette pauvre dépouille.[27]

As his journey through time approaches its end, accelerated by his symbolic painful illness through which, true to the "place assigned him through eternity" by Christ's side in the Garden of Olives, he helps expiate the evil wrought by the Fall, it begins to call forth an ever more abundant flow of grace, both within himself and in the beautiful figures we see springing up around him. Time itself becomes redemptive in the *Journal*. In contrast to the infernal cycles of repetition and return that mark the "satanic" works and that appear to pull the earth steadily back into the uncreated abyss, the movement traced through the diary is one of progress and growing abundance. In the continuity of earthly time made visible by the diary, every moment of the curé d'Ambricourt's life, even the most forsaken, reveals itself to be an integral part of a steadily unfolding process of creation and redemption. Every moment of desolation, as he passes through it and

[26] *Les Enfants humiliés*, p. 107.
[27] *Journal d'un curé de campagne*, p. 363.

suffers it humbly, without resisting it head on and thereby
letting its impact arrest him, turns over the inner soil of his
being more deeply and releases a new, hitherto unsuspected
spring of life.

As his simplicity becomes purer—

> . . . les gens du monde disent "les simples" comme ils disent
> "les humbles," avec le même sourire indulgent. Ils devraient
> dire: les rois.[28]

—his "infernal nights" of coldness and emptiness, which
reflect the "incomprehensible sterility" of satanic *ennui*,
flow into unexpectedly transparent, light-hearted mornings
which are like "a grace of God, a smile."[29] The violent
alternations, in which he has seen himself at first tossed
back and forth between moments of divine plenitude and
moments in which the abyss stares at him through his
empty hands, give way to a sustained sense of communion
in which this abyss placed between his natural poverty and
the infinite divine life by satanic hatred is overcome. Purged
of all delusion, his dream of Paradise assumes its true
dimensions: it becomes the vision of an earth redeemed by
the heavenly water in its own depths, and of a divine water
wedded to and become truly creative through earth. The
dream is freed of the last traces of a "maniac's dialogue
with his own shadow"[30] and becomes one with the mysteriously efficacious prayer of the saints, reopening the earth's
access to God:

> Par quel miracle ces demi-fous, prisonniers d'un rêve, ces
> dormeurs éveillés semblent-ils entrer plus avant chaque jour
> dans l'intelligence des misères d'autrui? Etrange rêve, singu-
> lier opium qui loin de replier l'individu sur lui-même, de
> l'isoler de ses semblables, le fait solidaire de tous, dans
> l'esprit de l'universelle charité! . . . cette sorte d'approfon-
> dissement intérieur ne ressemble à aucun autre. . . . au lieu

[28] *Ibid.*, p. 342.   [29] *Ibid.*, p. 282.   [30] *Ibid.*, p. 129.

de nous découvrir à mesure notre propre complexité il
aboutit à une soudaine et totale illumination. . . . il débouche
dans l'azur. . . .[31]

The last part of the *Journal* is a sober, yet deeply poetic
evocation of the "miracle of the empty hands," in which a
flawless interplay of grace and nature turns the curé
d'Ambricourt into a figure of ever-growing serenity and
youthfulness.

O merveille [he notes in his beloved diary], qu'on puisse
ainsi faire présent de ce qu'on ne possède pas soi-même, ô
doux miracle de nos mains vides![32]

Guided by the pedagogy of time, in the course of which he
finds himself stripped bare at every moment of all he has,
only to see the Father's gifts flow through him with greater
and greater abundance, he, alone among Bernanos' saints,
is allowed to share not only the agony of the Passion but
the transcendent joy of the Incarnation. His earthly journey towards death is depicted on the vital level of his own
consciousness of life and of himself as a steady, miraculous
progression from old age to youth. As the diary frees him
of his satanic double, both the narrow world of Ambricourt
and his own self emerge before his eyes as the bearers and
guardians of infinite inner richness, as a land of inexhaustible fountains.

Elles m'ont délivré du rêve [he says with overwhelming
gratitude of the diary's pages]. Ce n'est pas rien. Il est
possible, probable même, qu'elles me seront inutiles désormais. Dieu me comble de tant de grâces, et si inattendues,
si étranges! Je déborde de confiance et de paix.[33]

On all sides, the earth begins to give up its secrets to him.
Where at first, under the spell of his *vertige* of the infinite,
he could discern nothing but a dense opaqueness, mist, rain,
dust, and barrenness, he now discovers everywhere, waiting

[31] *Ibid.*, pp. 130, 131.   [32] *Ibid.*, p. 221.   [33] *Ibid.*, p. 307.

to be recognized and set free, an abundance of pure, untapped springs: in the countess, in Dr. Delbende, in Séraphita and Chantal, in Olivier de Mainville, in the humble little "poule" of his defrocked confrere. In a divine reversal, the village of Ambricourt itself, which has borne down on his too fluid, too purely transcendent dream with a crushing weight, now emerges before his clear glance, freed of all weight, in all the beauty of its true life:

> . . . on dirait que la limpidité de l'air lui enlève peu à peu toute pesanteur, et lorsque le soleil commence à décliner, on pourrait le croire suspendu dans le vide, il ne touche plus à la terre, il m'échappe, il s'envole. C'est moi qui me sens lourd, qui pèse d'un grand poids sur le sol. Parfois, l'illusion est telle que je regarde avec une sorte de terreur, une répulsion inexplicable, mes gros souliers. Que font-ils là, dans cette lumière?[34]

At last, in a unique development in Bernanos' works, the curé's limpid glance reaches into the depths of his own being and releases the most hidden spring of divine love, which finally reconciles him to himself. The affectionate, admiring glance of Olivier de Mainville gives him in a flash the revelation of his own youth. Suddenly he "recognizes" it and is able to forgive it its clumsiness and all the pain it has caused him, that pain which was the result not of any dereliction on its part but of the abyss between its immense expectations and its fragile resources.

> Je la voyais pour la première fois, je ne l'avais jamais vue. Elle était passée jadis—ainsi que passent près de nous tant d'étrangers dont nous eussions fait des frères, et qui s'éloignent sans retour.[35]

> . . . je la regarde sans méfiance. . . . Elle me regarde aussi, elle me pardonne. Accablé du sentiment de la maladresse foncière qui me rendait incapable d'aucun progrès, je prétendais exiger d'elle ce qu'elle ne pouvait donner, je la trouvais

---

[34] *Ibid.*, pp. 282–83.   [35] *Ibid.*, p. 287.

ridicule, j'en avais honte. Et maintenant, las tous deux de nos vaines querelles, nous pouvons nous asseoir au bord du chemin, respirer un moment, sans rien dire, la grande paix du soir où nous allons rentrer ensemble.[36]

The images which evoke this reconciliation are those of a limpid spring gushing forth and steeping the soul in freshness and new life;[37] and an earth so tenderly beautiful that having to part from it breaks his heart.

Le monde visible semblait s'écouler de moi avec une vitesse effrayante et dans un désordre d'images, non pas funèbres, mais au contraire toutes lumineuses, éblouissantes. Est-ce possible? L'ai-je donc tant aimé? me disais-je. Ces matins, ces soirs, ces routes. Ces routes changeantes, mystérieuses, ces routes pleines du pas des hommes. . . . Quel enfant pauvre, élevé dans leur poussière, ne leur a confié ses rêves? Elles les portent lentement, majestueusement, vers on ne sait quelles mers inconnues, ô grands fleuves de lumière et d'ombres qui portez les rêves des pauvres![38]

In the curé d'Ambricourt's life, the childhood dream of Paradise is redeemed from the status of a promise unattainable by way of any earthly path and becomes a reality in the midst of intense earthly suffering, right under his eyes. If he is saved from the satanic curse, able, that is to say, to cross the sea of death and enter the Father's Kingdom in so manifest a fashion, this is because his is, of all of Bernanos' saints', the most perfect poverty. Unlike the Abbé Chevance and even Chantal, of whom we really see only the component of grace, the heavenly water which flows through them, but who somehow fail to emerge in their earthly substance and fully to embrace the world, he is both infinitely supple and fluid in the Father's hands and at the same time a figure of poignant human emotions, and

[36] *Ibid.*, p. 357.
[37] Cf. epigraph to this chapter.
[38] *Journal d'un curé de campagne*, p. 336.

possibly above all, of humor. He is able to laugh at himself, as Bernanos was able to do, in so childlike, so truly innocent a way, that Satan has no chance left to laugh at him; for laughter dispells delusion, especially the most fatal one, the delusion of self-importance. In its loving acceptance of human frailty, it is so truly of this earth that no mirage of infinitude can prevail against it. In his final trial, as he attempts to prepare himself for his death, the anguish of which is almost overpowering, that humor assures him of the uselessness of aspiring to an exemplary death and reminds him that the death agony, above all, is the gift of self to the Father in all its humble imperfection.

> Je ne mourrai pas sans larmes. Alors que rien ne m'est plus étranger qu'une indifférence stoïque, pourquoi souhaiterais-je la mort des impassibles? Les héros de Plutarque m'inspirent tout ensemble de la peur et de l'ennui. Si j'entrais au paradis sous ce déguisement, il me semble que je ferais sourire jusqu'à mon ange gardien. Pourquoi m'inquiéter? Pourquoi prévoir? Si j'ai peur, je dirai: j'ai peur, sans honte. Que le premier regard du Seigneur, lorsque m'apparaîtra sa Sainte Face, soit donc un regard qui rassure![39]

[39] *Ibid.*, p. 360.

Bibliography

I. WORKS OF GEORGES BERNANOS (fiction, hagiography, and other works on which this essay is based directly).

Un Crime. Paris: Plon, 1935.

Dialogue d'ombres. Paris: Plon, 1955.

Dialogues des Carmélites. Paris: Editions du Seuil, 1949.

Les Enfants humiliés. Paris: Gallimard, 1949.

L'Imposture. Paris: Plon, 1927.

Jeanne relapse et sainte. Paris: Plon, 1934.

La Joie. Paris: Plon, 1929.

Journal d'un curé de campagne. Paris: Plon, 1936.

Un Mauvais Rêve. Paris: Plon, 1951.

Monsieur Ouine. Paris: Plon, 1946.

Nouvelle Histoire de Mouchette. Monaco: Editions du Rocher, 1946.

Saint Dominique. Paris: Gallimard, 1939.

Sous le Soleil de Satan. Paris: Plon, 1926.

153

II. MAJOR CRITICAL STUDIES OF BERNANOS.

BÉGUIN, ALBERT. *Georges Bernanos: Essais et témoignages.* Paris: Editions du Seuil, 1949.

————. *Bernanos par lui-même.* Paris: Editions du Seuil, 1954.

BUSH, WILLIAM. *Souffrance et expiation dans la pensée de Bernanos.* Paris: Lettres Modernes, 1961.

CHAIGNE, LOUIS. *Georges Bernanos.* Paris: Editions Universitaires, 1954.

ESTANG, LUC. *Présence de Bernanos.* Paris: Plon, 1947.

ESTÈVE, MICHEL. *Le Sens de l'amour dans les romans de Bernanos.* Paris: Lettres Modernes, 1960.

GAUCHER, GUY. *Le Thème de la mort dans les romans de Bernanos.* Paris: Lettres Modernes, 1955.

————. *Georges Bernanos.* Paris: Plon, 1961.

GILLESPIE, JESSIE LYNN. *Le Tragique dans l'oeuvre de Georges Bernanos.* Geneva: Librairie Droz, 1960.

HEBBLETHWAITE, PETER. *Bernanos.* ("Studies in Modern European Literature and Thought.") New York: Hillary House, 1965.

PICON, GAÉTAN. *Georges Bernanos.* Paris: R. Marin, 1948.

POULET, GEORGES. *Le point de départ.* ("Etudes sur le temps humain.") Paris: Plon, 1964.

URS VON BALTHASAR, HANS. *Bernanos.* Cologne and Olten: Jakob Hegner, 1954. [Also in French translation as *Le Chrétien Bernanos* (Paris: Editions du Seuil), 1956.]

THE POETIC

IMAGINATION OF

GEORGES BERNANOS

BY GERDA BLUMENTHAL

Georges Bernanos (1888-1948) is one of the most original and important French novelists of the twentieth century. In this study Gerda Blumenthal focuses attention on a neglected aspect of his work, namely, its powerful poetic substance.

Throughout Bernanos' works of fiction, from the early *Dialogues D' ombres* to the last and most complex novel, *Monsieur Ouine*, man's quest for Paradise is conceived poetically, as a gigantic contest of divorce and reconciliation between two elements, water and earth.

With great sensitivity, Miss Blumenthal explores the deep ambivalence of the Bernanosian water, which expresses the two spiritual poles between which the human earth is suspended in the novelist's universe and tossed back and forth: the hidden spirit of divine love,